IELTS *express*

Intermediate

r's Guide

Richard Hallows

Martin Lisboa

Mark Unwin

Australia • Canada • Mexico • Singapore • Spain • United Kingdom • United States

IELTS Express Intermediate, Teacher's Guide
Hallows / Lisboa / Unwin

Publisher: *Christopher Wenger*
Director of Product Development: *Anita Raducanu*
Director of Product Marketing: *Amy Mabley*
Editorial Manager: *Sean Bermingham*
Development Editor: *Derek Mackrell*
Contributing Writers: *Ranald Barnicot, Mark Harrison, Pamela Humphreys, Russell Whitehead*
Production Editor: *Tan Jin Hock*

International Marketing Manager: *Ian Martin*
Sr. Print Buyer: *Mary Beth Hennebury*
Project Manager: *Howard Middle/HM ELT Services*
Production Management: *Process ELT*
Copy Editor: *Katerina Mestheneou*
Compositor: *Process ELT*
Cover/Text Designer: *Studio Image & Photographic Art*
(www.studio-image.com)
Printer: *G. Canale & C S.p.a*

Printed in Italy.
1 2 3 4 5 6 7 8 9 10   09 08 07 06 05

For more information contact Thomson Learning, High Holborn House, 50/51 Bedford Row, London WC1R 4LR United Kingdom or Thomson ELT, 25 Thomson Place, Boston, Massachusetts 02210 USA. You can visit our web site at elt.thomson.com

For permission to use material from this text or product, submit a request online at
http://www.thomsonrights.com
Any additional questions about permissions can be submitted by e-mail to thomsonrights@thomson.com.

ISBN: 1-4130-0958-1

Author Acknowledgements
The authors would like to jointly thank Sean Bermingham and Derek Mackrell for their considerable creative input, hard work and sheer dedication to this project, Howard Middle, project consultant for his superb problem solving skills, and Chris Wenger the publisher for his good humour and showing us all a good time. We would also like to thank Loukas Ioannou and Georgia Zographou for their warm hospitality in Athens and help with development ideas for the book.

Martin: A big thank you to colleagues and students at the English Language Centre, London Metropolitan University for trialling material and offering sound advice and support. To my wife Manuela and my son Max, a very special thank you for tolerating me spending far too much time in front of the computer screen – without your support, good humour and inspiration, this book would have been impossible.

Richard: I'd like to thank my parents and friends, especially the Simons, who have supported me through this amazing project.

Mark: In addition to our wonderful editors and designers ... I'd like to thank my wife Sarah, my family, everyone whose brains I've picked over the last two years (they know who they are) and finally every student I've ever had in my class and every teacher whose class I've ever been in.

Contents

What is IELTS?

IELTS (International English Language Testing System) is a globally recognised English language exam, designed to assess the language ability of candidates who need to study or work where English is the language of communication. It is accepted by the majority of universities and further education colleges in the UK, Australia, Ireland, New Zealand, Canada and South Africa as well as a large number of institutions in the United States. It is recognised by professional bodies, immigration authorities and other government agencies. IELTS is jointly managed by: the University of Cambridge ESOL Examinations (Cambridge ESOL), the British Council and IDP: IELTS Australia.

IELTS is offered in two formats – Academic Training and General Training. All candidates take the same Listening and Speaking modules and there is an option of either Academic or General Training Reading and Writing modules. Academic Training is suitable for students wishing to enter an undergraduate or postgraduate study programme. General Training is suitable for candidates planning to undertake non-academic training, or work experience, or for immigration purposes. Further information about the exam can be obtained from the IELTS website www.ielts.org.

For a description of the four modules of the IELTS Exam, and what they contain, see the *IELTS Exam Overview* in the fold-out flap at the front of the *IELTS Express Intermediate Coursebook*.

How is IELTS scored and what are examiners looking for?

Each part of the IELTS exam is scored on a scale of 0 – 9. When candidates receive their results, they are given a breakdown of the band scores achieved in each of the four sections of the exam and a final band score, which is calculated as an average of the scores for the four separate sections.

For both Listening and Reading, one mark is awarded for each correct answer. The total number of marks is then converted into the above IELTS 9-band scale using a confidential method which can vary from test to test. Band scores may be reported as either full bands (e.g. 6) or half bands (e.g. 6.5).

The Writing and Speaking modules are assessed by trained examiners. At present, band scores for these two skills are given as full bands. However, in January 2007, a half band scale will be introduced. The exact marking criteria for the Speaking and Writing modules are confidential, but students are assessed on the following.

Writing

Writing Task 1 (Academic and General Training modules)
- **Task achievement:** the extent to which the candidate has performed the required task, using the minimum of 150 words.
- **Coherence and cohesion:** how clearly and fluently the message is communicated.
- **Lexical resource:** the range, accuracy and appropriacy of vocabulary employed by the candidate.
- **Grammatical range and accuracy:** how many different and appropriate structures are used by the candidate at sentence level.

Writing Task 2 (Academic and General Training modules). In addition to coherence and cohesion, lexical resource, and grammatical range and accuracy:
- **Task response:** This evaluates how well candidates formulate and develop an argument in response to the prompt given in the question. It also evaluates how well candidates' opinions are supported by evidence, which may be drawn from the candidates' own experience. Texts should be at least 150 words in length.

Speaking
- **Fluency and coherence:** The IELTS board identifies speech rate and speech continuity as the two major indicators of fluency. Logical sequencing of sentences, clear demarcation of stages of a discussion and use of cohesive devices (connectors, conjunctions, etc) are key indicators of coherence.
- **Lexical resource:** (determined as above). In addition, the IELTS board places importance on a candidate's ability to confidently get around a gap in their vocabulary by using alternative words.

▸ **Grammatical range and accuracy:** The IELTS board identifies sentence length and complexity, use of subordinate clauses, and range of sentence structures – and the extent to which a candidate may deploy these features to shift information focus – as major indicators of grammatical range. Accuracy is measured by 'the number of grammatical errors in a given amount of speech and the communicative effect of error'.

▸ **Pronunciation:** Factors here include the degree to which speech is unintelligible, the level of L1 interference and the amount of strain imposed on the listener.

For further information on these descriptors and the exam, please see www.ielts.org.

What are candidates' problems in each section?

Students may have a range of difficulties with different parts of the IELTS exam. These are explored more fully and a range of remedial strategies are detailed and practised throughout the *IELTS Express* series. However, common difficulties encountered in each part of the exam include the following:

Listening

Each recording is played once only and candidates are often required to write and listen simultaneously. There may be a range of accents employed, along with a fair amount of unknown vocabulary. Candidates may have difficulty in following an argument or line of thought, as in Listening Section 4 (Academic monologue). Candidates also need to be able to recognise numbers and, even though this is a listening exam, correct spelling is required in answers.

Reading (Academic and General Training)

Many candidates find this part quite challenging. Time is short – in the Academic Training module, candidates are required to read three long texts totalling up to 2,700 words in length and answer forty questions in only sixty minutes. Additionally, the texts are usually on topics which many candidates may find unfamiliar. Because of the nature of the content, many words may be unknown and recognising paraphrasing may be difficult. Candidates may also be inexperienced with some of the more uncommon question types, for example, labelling a flowchart.

Writing

Task 1 (Academic Training)

As well as having good language skills, candidates need to be able to analyse, select and order data. They need to be able to see general trends, identify key 'chunks' of information and exceptions to the main trends. Descriptions, such as those required by Task 1, requires quite complex sentence structure.

Task 1 (General Training)

Candidates may have problems identifying what information to include or not include in the letter. Structuring the letter or using the correct register and tone may also be problematic.

Task 2 (Academic Training and General Training)

Candidates may be asked to write a detailed and supported argument on a subject they may never have thought that much about or have any opinions on! Additionally, some students may not be that familiar with the discursive style of writing demanded by this task, preferring consensus rather than disagreement. Again, using the correct register may be a problem, as may be organising and developing a logical argument.

Speaking

The first section usually presents few difficulties to candidates, although many candidates need practice in extending their answers. The second part requires them to continue talking for over a minute – a daunting task for many, particularly when they are nervous. A lack of vocabulary is also a problem for many. Topics discussed in the final section may be quite 'abstract'. Again, candidates may feel they have limited ideas and vocabulary.

How can IELTS Express Intermediate help your students?

The comprehensive range of course components in the *IELTS Express* series makes it a complete preparation course for the IELTS exam. In the Coursebook, the main IELTS skills have been divided into discrete modular blocks, with two main skills per unit. You may decide that your students need help in all four IELTS papers, in which case, you could work through the Coursebook sequentially, doing Unit 1, which is Reading and Speaking, then Unit 2, which is Listening and Writing and so on. Alternatively, you can customise the course, focusing on one or two particular sections in which your students may need more practice. Furthermore, the Coursebooks focus on building skills in addition to exam practice.

Reading

All the major IELTS reading task types are covered in *IELTS Express Intermediate*. These Reading sections are aimed at both students taking the General Training module and the Academic Training module. Although General Training and Academic Training candidates take different reading exams, the task types are identical for both, and so are taught together in *IELTS Express Intermediate*.

Writing

Units 2 and 6 are aimed at students taking the Academic Training module and cover Task 1. Units 4 and 8 cover Task 2 of both General Training and Academic Training. For those students taking the General Training module, there are three additional General Training Writing units at the end of the book – two for Task 1 and one for Task 2.

Listening

The four sections of the Listening exam are covered in *IELTS Express Intermediate*. All major IELTS task types are introduced. All the recorded material is included on the *IELTS Express Intermediate* Audio CDs and Cassettes.

Speaking

The three sections of the IELTS Speaking exam are covered in detail in the speaking sections of *IELTS Express Intermediate*. For additional practice, the *IELTS Express Intermediate Speaking Video/DVD* shows students taking a simulated IELTS Speaking exam with an IELTS examiner. Each video provides commentary from the examiner, who explains the different sections of the exam and comments on the candidates' performance with particular reference to the skills practised in the Speaking units of the Coursebooks. See page 109 of this Teacher's Guide for photocopiable worksheets to accompany the *IELTS Express Intermediate Video/DVD*, and page 103 for guidance on how to use the video with your class.

The modular structure of the Coursebook allows freedom in lesson and timetable planning and helps the student to focus more attention on their weaker skills. This skills division allows the teacher to customise the course to best fit the needs of their students. The *IELTS Express Workbook* gives further skills practice and exam task practice, and also builds vocabulary and provides focus on key grammatical structures.

What are the components of the IELTS Express series?

There is a full set of *IELTS Express* components available at both Intermediate level (IELTS band score 4 – 5.5) and Upper intermediate level (IELTS band score 5 and above). These components include:

Coursebooks

Each Coursebook begins with an overview of the IELTS exam, followed by eight units with umbrella themes linked to common IELTS topics. At the back of the Intermediate book is a special set of units for those candidates taking the General Training module and in both levels of the Coursebook there is a full IELTS Practice test. There is also an answer key, model essays for the Writing exam tasks and listening scripts for all of the Listening and Speaking exercises. In order to maintain test validity, the answer key for the Practice test is found only in the Teacher's Guide. There are also sample answer sheets to use in the Reading and Listening sections of the Practice test. In the back flap of the book, there are handy reference sections containing useful language and structures for the Speaking and Writing papers.

Audio Cassettes/CDs

These contain recordings for the exercises in the Listening units and the Practice test Listening exam, as well as recordings of model candidates for each of the Speaking sections.

Workbooks

These complement the Coursebooks, emphasising language building through vocabulary and grammar sections, as well as providing extra skills and exam task practice. They are suitable for classroom or self-study use, and are accompanied by a separate **cassette or CD**, which provides additional listening and speaking practice.

Teacher's Guides

These guides provide detailed unit notes with guidance on how to teach the activities as well as suggestions to extend the tasks and deal with anticipated problems. In addition, there are guidance notes on how to support weaker students (indicated by the *Support* heading) and to challenge stronger ones (indicated by the *Challenge* heading). These Teacher's Guides are designed to be suitable for experienced teachers of IELTS, as well as for teachers who are unfamiliar with the exam.

Speaking Videos/DVDs

These videos (also available on DVD) show students taking a simulated IELTS Speaking exam with an IELTS examiner. Each video provides commentary from the examiner, who explains the different sections of the exam and comments on the candidates' performance, with particular reference to the skills practised in the Speaking units of the Coursebooks. See page 109 for photocopiable worksheets to accompany the video, and page 103 for guidance on how to use the video with your class.

As part of the *Thomson Exam Essential* series, the *IELTS Express* package is further complemented by an *IELTS Practice Tests* book which provides six full Academic Module practice tests and additional writing and reading material for the General Training modules. The practice tests provide both guided and non-guided practice.

How can you use IELTS Express with your class?

Identify which components of the course your students need. *IELTS Express* has been designed to work flexibly to provide a range of courses of differing length and/or level.

For a 30-hour course

Each Coursebook provides a minimum core of 30 to 40 hours class time. That's a good length for a week-long intensive IELTS preparation course. Each skills section takes around 2 hours to cover. Each unit takes around 4 hours. The 8 units in the book will provide around 32 hours of material. The Practice test will take at least $2\frac{1}{2}$ to 3 hours, plus the Speaking exam, which is around 15 minutes per student if carried out individually. (See page 94 for other options for administering the Speaking exam.)

For 60 hours at a single level

Using the Workbook and Speaking Video, along with the video exercises in class will add a further 30 to 40 hours.

For 60 hours, covering two levels

For fast-track exam preparation courses over two levels, you could use both levels of the *IELTS Express Coursebook*, having students complete the Workbooks at home.

For 90+ hour courses

For longer IELTS exam preparation over two levels, using all the components at both levels, provides at least 90 hours of material – sufficient for a full-length IELTS foundation course lasting an academic year.

How do you teach a unit of IELTS Express?

Each unit of the Coursebook covers a broad IELTS-related theme and contains two exam sections. The first section looks at a receptive skill (reading or listening) and the second, a productive skill (speaking or writing). Each section should take around 2 hours, although this will depend on how quickly your students work. Slower groups can be coached to work faster by giving them a set time to finish a particular task. Time constraints are a real problem in the IELTS exam, particularly in the Reading and Writing modules and so you should encourage your students to increase their speed of working wherever possible. The lesson notes in this Teacher's Guide also contain suggested extension activities to give further practice. Adopting these variations will add time to your lesson.

Unit sections

Each unit section (Reading, Speaking, Listening and Writing) has been carefully constructed to introduce key exam skills, develop those skills, relate those skills to a specific exam task-type and finally, give students the opportunity to practise these new skills on a typical exam graded task.

A typical unit section consists of the following elements:

Unit number and exam section: appearing in the outer top corners of each page of each section, exam section boxes are colour coded, e.g. Reading is always blue, Speaking always green, etc.

Opening photographs: these provide a clear visual focus to begin each section and theme.

Introduction: this introduces the topic through discussion questions and presentation of target vocabulary.

Skills development exercises: using graded tasks, these exercises introduce and give practice in key IELTS sub-skills, for example, skimming and scanning, identifying a general trend, identifying paraphrase, etc.

'In the exam' box: this box, at the bottom of the first page of a skills section, is a key element of *IELTS Express,* enabling students to relate the skills practised in each section to the exam as a whole. It offers a straightforward description of aspects of the exam and details one or two task-types found in the exam.

'Express tip' box: these boxes, which appear in the margin at irregular intervals throughout a unit, give useful tips on exam strategy.

'For this task' box: this box precedes an exam practice task. It acts to relate a set of skills to a specific exam task-type. In other words, it tells students how to apply their newly acquired skills to the following set of exam practice questions.

Exam practice: each section ends with an exam practice task, giving students the opportunity to try out their new skills. Exam practice tasks are indicated by a circular icon in the margin beside the instructions, e.g.

Other icons: a headphone icon in the Listening and Speaking sections, e.g. 🎧 indicates that the teacher should use an audio component at this stage. The recording number is displayed in a coloured lozenge beside the icon, e.g. **1.1** .

Using the unit notes

Each section of the Coursebook has a corresponding set of notes in this Teacher's Guide, with suggestions and advice on how to teach that section. A typical set of notes will have the following elements and structure:

Title: unit number, theme, skill

Section aims: this provides a clear description of the main objectives of each skills section.

Each subsequent exercise contains:

Aims: a detailed description of the purpose of each exercise.

Procedure: a step-by-step guide on how to teach a particular exercise. It includes notes on introducing the theme or task, pre-teaching vocabulary, grouping students, anticipating problems, timing exercises, staging listening exercises, using the various 'boxes' in the Coursebook, eliciting feedback and checking answers, etc.

Answer key: the answer key provides explanations as to why a particular answer is correct, and why others are incorrect.

Listening script: in addition to the listening scripts at the back of the Coursebook, the Listening and Speaking listening scripts are provided again for convenience. For each question, the relevant section(s) of the script is underlined.

Support: this section gives advice on how to support those students who find a particular exercise challenging.

Challenge: this offers suggestions on how to stretch those students who find a particular exercise relatively easy.

Extension activities: *IELTS Express* is primarily designed as a fast-track exam preparation course, but if you feel your students would benefit from further practice in a particular area or if you simply find yourself with lesson time left over and you need extra material, then ideas for additional exercises are provided for many of the exercises.

For guidance on how to administer and mark the practice test, see the introduction to the practice test on page 93.

Studying Overseas

Section aims:
- To develop an awareness of the reading skills of skimming and scanning.
- To introduce the idea of predicting the content of a text from titles, summary paragraphs and subheadings.
- To practise a number of task types – short-answer questions; classification; true/false/not given.

1 Introduction

Aim: To introduce the topic of studying abroad and to act as a lead-in to the reading.

- Put the students into pairs or small groups to discuss the questions among themselves. Depending on your class size, you could turn this into an open class discussion, or have your students report back to another pair or group.

In the exam

Draw the students' attention to the information outlining the structure and content of the Reading module of the exam. The information focuses on the differences and similarities between the Academic module and the General Training module.

2 Skimming and scanning

Aims: To explain what skimming and scanning are and what they are used for.

To provide practice in skimming and scanning.

A ▸ Tell the students what skimming and scanning are. Explain that we skim to get 'the gist' of the text, i.e. the overall general meaning. For example, we might skim a long text to get an overall impression of it before deciding if we want to read any parts in detail. Scanning, on the other hand, helps us to pick out specific details – it is especially useful for finding names and numbers. In many ways, scanning is not what we conventionally think of as reading at all. Give an example of students looking at a web page and looking for an icon to click. E.g. if they are making a purchase, they might be looking for the shopping cart symbol – so they scan the page for it.
- Have the students complete this task alone. They should read situations 1–4, decide if each one involves skimming or scanning and tick the correct box.

▸ Have the students compare their answers with a partner before you check the answers as a class.

ANSWER KEY

This is the first activity in the book for which answers are provided. Draw your students' attention to the Answer key at the back of the Coursebook (page 109), but stress that they shouldn't look at the answers to an activity before completing it in class.

1 Answer: scan
Note You do not look over the whole page to get an impression of the TV programming for the evening – you want to know what's on now, so you scan for the correct time of day and read only that information.

2 Answer: scan
Note You aren't interested in looking at the trains for the whole day – you don't want to get a general impression of the train timetabling. You want to know what train is running at a specific time and so you scan the times until you find the hour you are looking for, then you read more closely.

3 Answer: skim
Note You skim the whole article to get an impression of the overall content. This will help you decide if you need to read a section again more carefully.

4 Answer: skim
Note You want to appear to have read the report, so you skim it to get a general impression of the text – although you won't know any of the details!

Extension: *Scanning race*

Aim: To provide further scanning practice, using a television guide.

Preparation
▸ Make one copy of a television guide for every group of students.
▸ Make a list of questions to ask the students, e.g. *I really enjoy gardening, what can I watch tonight?* or *How many films are on tonight?* The number of questions you write will depend on how much time you wish the activity to take.

Procedure

▸ Put the class into groups of 3–5 students.

▸ Give one copy of the television guide to each group. Explain that you are going to ask them questions – like a quiz – about the television guide and that they must work in their groups to try to find the answers as quickly as possible. Tell them to put their hands up as soon as they know the answer and that the first group to answer each question correctly receives one point. Keep track of each group's score on the board.

Extension: *Newspaper headline matching*

Aim: *To provide further skimming practice, using short newspaper articles.*

Preparation

▸ Choose between 5 and 10 short newspaper articles. The number of articles you choose will depend on how much time you wish the activity to take.

▸ Cut the headlines off the articles, stick them onto a sheet of paper and stick all the articles, minus their headlines, onto another sheet of paper, making sure that you mix up the order of either the headlines or the articles.

▸ Make one copy of each sheet for every group of students. To ensure that this activity focuses more on skimming than scanning, choose articles with headlines that don't contain obvious clues like names or places.

Procedure

▸ Put the class into groups of 3–5 students.

▸ Give one copy of each sheet to every group.

▸ Tell the students to match each headline to the correct article by skimming the articles for the main idea. Tell them that it is a race and that they should work as quickly as possible. This will make the students skim the articles rather than read them carefully.

B ▸ Tell the students they have to identify the main idea of the article by skimming the text and then decide which of the choices 1–3 best describes the main idea of the text.

▸ Stress that they are not expected to read or understand every word.

▸ Have the students read the choices 1–3, skim the article for thirty seconds and then circle the choice 1,

2 or 3 they think is correct.

▸ Be strict with the time limit, encouraging the students to skim the text, even though it may seem difficult at first.

▸ Check the answers as a class. Explain why the incorrect answers are wrong.

ANSWER KEY

Answer: 3
Note English is the most widely used language in the world. 1 and 2 are incorrect because they only focus on specific aspects of the text, rather than the text as a whole.

Express tip

Read out the advice in this box while students follow in their books. As this is the first *express tip* box in the book, explain to the students that these boxes contain useful tips about the exam.

C ▸ Tell the students that numbers can 'jump out' of a text. Use the number '45' in the text to exemplify this. Have the students shout out or put their hands up when they have found this number.

▸ Ask the students if they remember what the numbers 70% and 50% in the text refer to. Draw their attention to the references.

▸ Have the students scan the text to find the numbers 70% and 50%. Once they have found the numbers, have them read the whole sentence around each one so that they can match the numbers to the references.

▸ Check the answers as a class.

ANSWER KEY

over 70%: the amount of mail written in English
over 50%: the amount of business done in English

Challenge

▸ Ask the students to find the other numbers in the text and identify what they refer to.

ANSWER KEY

300 million: native speakers of English, and people who use it as a foreign language

a billion: people who use English as a foreign language. (This one is slightly trickier as the number is spelled out, rather than written in numerals.)

45: the number of countries in which English is the official or co-official language

Extension: *Reading the business news*

Aim: *To provide further scanning practice, using newspaper business articles.*

Preparation

▸ Choose several articles from newspaper business pages that contain statistics. The number of articles you choose will depend on how much time you wish the activity to take.

▸ Make a copy of each article for every student or every pair of students.

▸ On your copy, circle or highlight all the numbers that appear in the texts.

▸ If you follow the alternative suggestion at the end of this activity, make a list of sentences which refer to the numbers in the articles.

Procedure

▸ Put the students into pairs or have them work alone. Write the numbers you selected from the texts on the board. Make sure the numbers are in random order.

▸ Tell the students they have to locate each number on the board by scanning the articles, and that it is a race. This will encourage them to skim the articles rather than read them carefully.

▸ Tell the students to circle the numbers as they find them. The first student or pair of students to find all the numbers should shout out or put up their hands. When all the students have found all the numbers, have them write sentences explaining what the numbers refer to. Alternatively, you can write your list of sentences on the board and have the students match the numbers to the information.

3 Predicting content

Aims: To introduce the idea of predicting the content of a text by using information in the title, the summary paragraph and any subheadings.

To introduce students to 'surveying' the text to get an overall impression of it, by looking at only the first sentence in each paragraph. This will help to increase their reading speed.

A ▸ Introduce this activity by asking the students *When you read a newspaper, how do you decide which stories to read?* Establish that they base their decision on looking at the headlines and predicting what the story will be about.

▸ Have the students read the main heading, summary paragraph (in blue) and paragraph headings to predict the content of the text.

▸ Ask them to choose which of the statements 1, 2 or 3 they think best describes the text.
Don't allow the students to check their answers yet – this will be done after they have done activity B.

B ▸ Have the students skim the text to decide if the predictions they made in A are correct. Point out that the first sentence of each paragraph is often the topic sentence, i.e. it contains the main idea of the paragraph.

▸ Be strict with the time limit, encouraging the students to skim. Call out the time every 30 seconds to encourage students to pick up the pace.

▸ Check the answer to 3A as a class.

ANSWER KEY

Answer: 3
Note 1 is incorrect because, even though the article mentions universities, the focus is on the countries rather than the institutions. **2** is incorrect because the article is about five countries equally, rather than just the UK.

Extension: *Newspaper article prediction*

Aim: *To provide further prediction practice, using newspaper article headlines.*

Preparation

▸ Ask the students to choose an article from an English language newspaper and bring it to class. If they have no access to English language newspapers, they can easily get one from the Internet if they have access, or you could provide the newspaper yourself.

▸ It's probably a good idea for you to have a couple of articles in reserve, in case any of the students have difficulties or forget to bring their articles.

Procedure

▸ Have the students work in pairs and take turns doing the task.

▸ Each student shows the article they have chosen to their partner. Their partner then makes predictions about the content of the article by looking only at the headline and any subheadings.

▸ The student who chose the article should then explain what the headline means and confirm or correct the other student's guesses.

▸ Have the students change partners for additional practice.

Support

▸ After students have skimmed the text, allow them to read it again more carefully and explain any difficult vocabulary. As exercise 3B is intended to practise skimming rather than reading for detail, don't pre-teach this vocabulary before they skim. Stress that it isn't necessary to understand every word in the passage to answer question 3A.

▸ The following items could be singled out for attention:

migration   founded   liberty   freedom   values concluded   survey   based on   paramount multi-lingual   think for yourself   lower living costs literature   a good reputation   dynamism

▸ Remind the students that they will not usually have the advantage when doing exam practice tasks of having been through difficult vocabulary beforehand.

4 Short-answer questions

Aim: To introduce short-answer questions as a task type.

For this task

▸ Read the information in the *For this task* box aloud and have the students follow in their books. Stress that they have to use the correct number of words – the amount is stated in the exam rubric – and that they cannot change the form of the words at all. Emphasise that the students will need to use the scanning techniques practised earlier.

Exam practice

▸ This is the first exam practice task in the book. Point out to the students that these exam practice tasks are identified by the exam practice stamp.

▸ Tell the students that for questions 1–5 they should scan the text for the names of countries to locate the right sections of text. Stress that scanning will enable them to save time, even if it feels a strange way to read at the moment.

▸ Have the students work alone to answer questions 1–5. Remind them that in the exam, they need to answer 40 reading questions in an hour, so limit their time here to less than 10 minutes.

▸ Check the answers as a class.

ANSWER KEY

I Answer: (a) foundation course
Note 'Some UK institutions offer a foundation course ... to prepare international students ... '

2 Answer: (the) British system –
Note 'New Zealand's highly respected educational programmes are based on the British system.'

3 Answer: liberty (and) freedom
Note ' ... liberty and freedom are probably the most important ... '

4 Answer: community college courses
Note '... from two-year community college courses ... '

5 Answer: (the) United Nations
Note 'Surveys conducted by the United Nations have repeatedly found Canada to be among the top three places in the world to live in.'

5 Classification

Aims: To introduce classification as a task type.

To give students the opportunity to consolidate the skills introduced so far in this section.

For this task

▸ Read the information in the *For this task* box aloud and have students follow in their books.

▸ Make sure students are clear on what is meant by paraphrase.

▸ Emphasise that students should use the skimming and scanning techniques practised earlier.

Exam practice

▸ Have the students work alone to answer questions 6–10.

▸ Check the answers as a class.

ANSWER KEY

6 Answer: US
Note 'With 50 states all offering a huge range of different types of institutions ... '

7 Answer: AU
Note ' ... Australian institutions have a particularly strong reputation for research into the environment ... '

8 Answer: UK
Note 'Many students are attracted to Britain by its long history of literature, from Chaucer and Shakespeare to Bridget Jones and Harry Potter.'

9 Answer: US
Note 'American students are therefore expected to think independently ...'

10 Answer: NZ
Note 'Low living costs and a high standard of living also make life here very appealing.'

Support

▸ For questions 6–10, ask the students to identify which words in each question are paraphrased in the text. E.g. in question 6 'enormous choice' refers to 'huge range' and 'colleges and universities' refers to 'institutions'.

ANSWER KEY

7 'universities' refers to 'institutions'; 'famous' refers to 'have a particularly strong reputation'; 'environmental studies' refers to 'research into the environment'

8 'famous authors' refers to 'Chaucer and Shakespeare to Bridget Jones and Harry Potter'

9 'should' refers to 'are ... expected to'; 'think for themselves' refers to 'think independently'

10 'not a very expensive place to live in' refers to 'low living costs'

Express tip

Read out the advice in this box while students follow in their books.
Explain the information in the box by drawing attention to the categories of countries above questions 6–10, which are in alphabetical order, although this isn't the order in which the countries are presented in the text.

Extension: *Paraphrasing*

Aim: To introduce the concept of paraphrasing. This is introduced in more detail in Unit 2.

Preparation

▸ On one sheet of paper, write down all the words and phrases on the left of the lists. Label this sheet 'A'. On another, write all the words and phrases on the right. Make sure you mix up the order of the items. Label this sheet 'B'.
▸ Make one copy of each sheet for every student or every pair of students.

Group 1

1 big — *a* large
2 house — *b* home
3 clever — *c* intelligent
4 beautiful — *d* pretty
5 very hot — *e* boiling
6 holiday — *f* vacation

Group 2

1 It was a very cosmopolitan city. — *a* Its citizens came from around the world.
2 It isn't very expensive. — *b* The cost of living is very reasonable.
3 It has a strong reputation for discipline. — *c* It is well known for being strict.
4 They are publicly-funded. — *d* They are state-financed.

Group 3

1 He lived there for ages and ages. — *a* He was a resident for a very long time.
2 It was absolutely gorgeous! — *b* It was beautiful.
3 It was bit tricky. — *c* It was quite difficult.

Group 4

1 He had a degree in Accountancy. — *a* He was a qualified accountant.
2 Many of the people were very poor. — *b* Poverty was a major problem.
3 They never tell the truth. — *c* What they say is never true.

Procedure

▸ Put the class in pairs or have them work alone. Ask the students to match the items on sheet 'A' with those on sheet 'B'.

6 True/False/Not Given

Aims: To introduce True/False/Not Given questions as a task type.

To give students the opportunity to further consolidate the skills introduced in this section.

For this task

▸ Have the students read the information in the *For this task* box. As students find this task type quite challenging, spend extra time clarifying the difference between true, false and not given – particularly differentiating between the false and not given answers. Students may waste time looking for a true or false answer, when in fact it is not given.

▸ Remind the students that they must only use the information in the text, not their own personal knowledge – sometimes students think something is true based on their own knowledge, when in fact they can't find it in the text.

Exam practice

▸ Have the students answer questions 11–15.
▸ Check the answers as a class, explaining why each answer was correct.

ANSWER KEY

11 Answer: False
Note ' … its high level of public safety … '

12 Answer: True
Note 'Academically speaking, most of the national, publicly-funded universities are of similarly high standard.'

13 Answer: True
Note ' … you'll find a university system with one of the best reputations in the world.'

14 Answer: Not Given
Note Although the text mentions that British universities have a good reputation, it doesn't say anything about their practical element.

15 Answer: Not Given
Note The text mentions Canada as being 'among the top three places in the world to live in' and mentions three cities as being 'world class'. It does not, however, talk about this with regard to universities. Point out that students need to read very carefully when dealing with this task type.

1

Section aims:
▸ To help students sound more fluent by encouraging them to extend their responses, and avoid short answers, particularly by asking themselves follow-up questions.
▸ To introduce the type of questions students might encounter in Part 1 of the Speaking exam and give them the opportunity to develop their own answers.
▸ To practise Part 1 of the Speaking exam: Introduction and interview.

1 Introduction

Aim: To introduce students to the types of everyday questions they are likely to be asked in Part 1 of the Speaking exam.

A ▸ Focus the students' attention on the photos. Establish that the people in the photos are meeting each other for the first time.

▸ Put the students in pairs and have them make a list of typical questions the people might be asking each other. When the students have finished their lists, ask them to tell you the questions they thought of and write them on the board. The list should include questions such as:

What's your name?

Where do you come from?

Do you live in a town or the country? What's it like?

What's your job? What do you do for a living? Do you have a job?

Do you have any brothers or sisters? Do you get on with them?

What do you do in your free time?

Why are you taking IELTS? What do you plan after the course? Do you plan to study abroad?

Do you enjoy studying English?

B ▸ Have the students ask each other the questions on their list. Then they should change partners and talk to someone else, so they get the opportunity to ask and answer several times, therefore increasing their confidence and giving them the chance to develop their answers. If it is a relatively new group, it will also give them a chance to get to know each other a little.

Extension: *Role card introductions*

Aim: *To give further practice in introductions by having students adopt a new identity.*

Preparation
▸ Make one role card for each student in the class. The cards, which can be just small pieces of paper, should contain the names and a few personal details of either famous or fictitious people. If you don't have time to prepare cards, just have students come up with their own identities.

Procedure
▸ Follow the procedure of 1B, but this time students assume the identity written on the role cards you give them. If students avoid the question *What's your name?*, this can become a guessing activity, where students try to guess the identity of their partner. Have the students change partners and repeat the activity.

In the exam
▸ Read the information in the *In the exam* box aloud and have students follow. Take some time to go through the assessment criteria.

▸ Explain that 'fluency' means speaking without too much hesitation, and 'coherence' means speaking with a logical flow, so one idea flows into the next and the speaker has no problems following your thoughts. 'Vocabulary range' refers to how many different and 'high level' (lower frequency) words the speaker uses. 'Grammatical range and accuracy' refers to how many grammatical structures the speaker uses and if these structures are used accurately.

▸ Explain that students are not assessed on whether their pronunciation is that of a native speaker, but instead, on how clearly they are able to communicate.

▸ Stress that this part of the exam is to give students an opportunity to relax and be prepared for later stages. Nerves clearly can be a problem in the

Speaking exam, so spend time reassuring the students that the first part is nothing to worry about – especially if they have thought of answers beforehand. However, it is important that students don't learn their responses by heart because examiners will recognise rote responses and the students will lose marks. Of course, there are only so many ways students can answer *Where do you live?* or *What's your name?* The important thing is that they listen carefully to the examiner's question so they answer the question the examiner actually asks, rather than the one they think the examiner is asking.

2 Answering questions about yourself

Aim: To help students to predict questions and answers for Part 1 of the Speaking exam and provide them with expressions to help them sound more natural when they speak.

A ▸ Explain to the students that they are going to read six dialogues from which the first line has been removed. Ask them to read the six B lines – the responses.

▸ Have the students predict questions which would produce the answers in 1–6. Students should not write in their books until they have listened for the answers in B. For the moment, tell students to ignore the spaces (a–f).

B ▸ Play the recording and ask the students to check if their predictions were correct.

▸ Have them write down the actual questions that were asked in 1–6.

ANSWER KEY

1 Do you enjoy studying English?
2 What do you do in your free time?
3 Do you plan to study abroad?
4 Do you have any brothers or sisters?
5 What's your job?
6 Where do you live?

1.1 LISTENING SCRIPT

This is the first recording in the course. Draw students' attention to the listening scripts at the back of the Coursebook (page 115), but stress that they should not read them before they've heard the recording.

1

A: <u>Do you enjoy studying English?</u>

B: <u>I'm afraid</u> I don't like it very much. I think it's really difficult, especially the grammar.

2

A: <u>What do you do in your free time?</u>

B: <u>It depends</u>. I often go out with my friends, but sometimes I enjoy just reading in my room.

3

A: <u>Do you plan to study abroad?</u>

B: I haven't really decided yet. <u>I guess</u> I'd like to one day, maybe in Canada or Australia.

4

A: <u>Do you have any brothers or sisters?</u>

B: <u>Well,</u> I have one brother and one sister.

5

A: <u>What's your job?</u>

B: I have a part-time job in a local shop. <u>In fact</u>, I've worked there for more than three years.

6

A: <u>Where do you live?</u>

B: <u>Actually</u>, my parents moved around a lot and I've lived in many cities. Now I live in Osaka.

C ▸ Tell the students that they are going to hear the recording again and that they should listen for the missing words and expressions (a–f) in speaker B's responses. If you have a strong class, elicit any answers that they remember.

▸ Play the recording again and have the students fill in the spaces (a–f) with the missing words and expressions.

▸ Check the answers as a class.

ANSWER KEY

a I'm afraid; **b** It depends; **c** I guess; **d** Well; **e** In fact; **f** Actually

---

D ‣ Check that students understand what each of the functions means.

‣ Have them write the words and expressions in the correct part of the table next to the appropriate function.

Express tip

Read out the advice in the box while students follow in their books. Explain that these expressions, when used appropriately, can help candidates sound more fluent. Encourage your class to use expressions like these when speaking.

E ‣ Put the students into pairs or small groups.
Have the students personalise the questions and answers 1–6 and use the expressions from the table in D.

3 Extending your responses

Aim: To help students develop longer responses and avoid one-word answers, something that will earn them a lot of credit from the examiner.

A ‣ Explain to the students that extending their responses is very important in the Speaking exam. Write *Do you like … ?* on the board and have students use it to ask you various questions.

‣ Answer *Yes* or *No* and then ask them if your answers were interesting.

‣ Have students ask you their questions again, but this time extend your responses, e.g. *Yeah, I think it's great; I've always wanted to …* etc. Refer them to the example in the Coursebook.

B ‣ Put the students into pairs and write the question *Do you plan to study abroad?* on the board. Direct the students' attention to the follow-up questions in the Coursebook and ask them to think of some more follow-up questions. Possibilities include:
What are some of the problems (or challenges) that you will face?
What are the benefits of studying abroad?
How will it be different from studying in your country?

‣ Write the students' questions on the board.
Have the students ask the questions to as many other students as possible. Encourage them to extend their responses in a different way each time they answer the questions.

C ‣ Do the first question with the class and write the following notes on the board.
No / only child / would like an elder brother
Yes / elder sister / get on well

‣ Have the students complete the exercise and then go through possible answers with the class as a whole before you listen to the recording in D.

Express tip

Read out the advice in this box while students follow in their books. Stress to students how important it is to use these linking words to join their sentences together in order to sound fluent. Throughout the rest of the unit, encourage your class to use these expressions when speaking.

D ‣ Have students listen to the same questions being answered and ask them to write down the keywords regarding the extra information the student supplied in their answer. This should enable students to judge how well developed their own answers are and, if they need to, extend them further.

ANSWER KEY

1 Suggested keywords

1 good relationship, shared a room, argued, fight
2 before that, studying in Ireland, for two years, living in countryside, get used to London eventually, takes time to adjust
3 sports, team sports, cricket, baseball, soccer, football
4 speaking with friends, reading, writing, vocabulary, learning, improve
5 quit, working, nurse, dentist
6 go to Sydney, study business, get a degree

2 Suggested follow-up questions

1 How do you get on with your sister? What is your relationship like? Are you close?
2 Where did you live before? How long did you live there? Did you like it? Do you like where you live now?
3 What sports do you like? What sports would you like to play?
4 What areas of English do you like? What is difficult? Are you happy with your progress?
5 What did you use to do? How long did you do that job? What job would you like to do in the future? Why?
6 Where do you want to go? What are you going to study? Why did you choose that country?

LISTENING SCRIPT

1

A: Yes, I have one sister. She's older than me. We have quite a good relationship now, but when I was younger it was different – not so good. We had to share a room and sometimes we argued about clothes and CDs – things like that. I guess that it's normal to fight a little with your sister.

2

B: Now I'm living in London, but before that I was studying in Ireland – for 2 years. Actually, it was great. I was living in the countryside and it was very peaceful. Not like London – it's so busy and noisy! I guess I'll get used to London eventually – it just takes time to adjust, doesn't it?

3

C: I enjoy playing most sports – especially team sports. Actually, I'm interested in learning the rules of cricket. It seems difficult to understand but I'd like to try it. I played baseball in Japan and I think it's similar. Also, I like playing soccer too, errr, you say football, don't you? But in fact ...

4

D: It depends. I enjoy speaking with my friends, but reading and writing I find difficult. Also, I have problems with vocabulary – I don't have enough! I've only been learning for one year, so I think I will continue to improve – I hope so.

5

E: Actually, I quit it last month. I was working as a nurse for a very long time, but now I want to study further because in the future I'd like to become a dentist. I'm not sure why I want to do this – most people think I'm crazy, but teeth have always been very interesting to me.

6

F: Yeah, I want to go to Sydney in Australia. I want to study business there so I can run my father's business. But, actually, I'm more interested in Australia because the sun and the surfing is good and it's one of my hobbies. I will study hard too. I must work hard to get a degree in business – and then go to the beach.

4 Introduction and interview

Aim: To provide a full Speaking Part 1 practice interview, where students can consolidate the skills introduced in the unit.

For this task

▸ Go through the *For this task* box with the students. Remind them to extend their answers and use the expressions and linking words given as examples to make them sound more natural when they speak.

Exam practice

▸ Put the students into pairs. Assign one student in each pair to be student A and the other to be student B.
▸ Advise the student acting as examiner to listen carefully as he or she will be giving feedback on his or her partner's performance. Allow 4–5 minutes for the activity. Allow student B 1–2 minutes to speak.
▸ After student B has finished talking, student A should give him or her feedback. Students should then change roles.
▸ If the students need more practice, have them find a different partner and repeat the activity.

IELTS Express Speaking Video

▸ If you are using the *Speaking Video* which accompanies *IELTS Express*, Section 1 – Overview and Section 2 – Part 1 of the video relate to the content of this unit.
▸ It would be helpful to show the Overview before this lesson to give students a general idea of the content and format of the IELTS Speaking exam. The Part 1 section of the video could be shown at the end of the lesson to provide a recap and demonstration of the material covered in this unit.

For more information on the IELTS Express Speaking Video and how to integrate it into your lessons, see page 103.

Shopping and the Internet

LISTENING

1 Introduction

Aims: To introduce the topics of shopping and technology.

To encourage students to think about different kinds of forms and the language needed to complete them.

▶ Draw students' attention to the four photographs. Ask the class if they can identify the item in photograph A. Elicit suggestions.
▶ Read the questions in the introduction aloud to the class and then have students discuss the questions in pairs or small groups for a few minutes.
▶ Gather some group feedback, checking answers, vocabulary and pronunciation.

ANSWER KEY

A mobile phone (or cell phone)

B digital camera

C radio

D (desktop) computer

A customer may ask the sales assistant:'How much is it? How much does it cost? Who is it made by? Does it take batteries? If I don't like it, can I bring it back?' etc.

The sales assistant may ask the customer 'Is it a present, or is it for you? Do you prefer a particular brand or model? How much do you want to spend?'

Forms may include: insurance (extended guarantee or warranty); hire purchase agreements (credit).

The customer may be asked for the following information depending on which type of form they are completing: name, contact details: address, phone number, email address, date of birth, occupation, marital status, bank details, passport number, ID, etc.

In the exam
Before reading through this, tell your students to close their books and ask them what they know about the Listening exam in terms of: length, number of sections, difference between sections, the nature of Section 1.

Ask them to discuss these questions in pairs and then check their answers by reading this box. Discuss answers as a class.

2 Imagining the situation and language

Aims: To introduce the students to the introductory sentence which precedes an IELTS Listening task and provides a context for it.

To encourage students to predict the kind of language they will hear in a particular listening task by imagining the situation after hearing the introduction.

A ▶ Write *You will hear a man enquiring about buying a camera* in big letters in the middle of the board. Put a circle round it and four arrows radiating away from it. Label these arrows: *place; people; functional language; topic related language*.
▶ Explain that by 'functional language', we mean things like asking for information, giving information, checking understanding, etc. By 'topic related', we mean language which is only used when talking about a particular thing. Refer back to the questions the class came up with in the introduction and have students decide which language is functional and which is topic related.
▶ Now work through the questions in the Coursebook, writing the suggestions made at the end of the relevant arrow.

Express tip
Read out the advice in this box while students follow in their books. Remind students that in the exam they are given a short pause to read the questions after hearing the introductory sentence. Stress that using this time to think about the situation and language they will hear will help them in the task which follows.

B
- Tell the students they will now hear the situation they discussed in A.
- Ask them to listen and note if their predictions about the situation were correct. Tell them to write down any topic related language they hear which they hadn't predicted.
- Play recording 2.1.
- Go through their answers as a class and write any new vocabulary on the board.

ANSWER KEY

Topic related vocabulary may include: camera, digital, zoom, lens, pictures, photos and memory.

2.1 **LISTENING SCRIPT**

(C = Customer; SA = Shop assistant)

C: Excuse me?

SA: Yes. Can I help you?

C: I want to buy a new camera.

SA: Certainly. Digital or film?

C: Digital.

SA: Any particular make or model?

C: No ... I've just started looking, actually.

SA: Well, this is the EazeeShot ZX. As you can see, it has a zoom lens ...

C: Mm. Looks good!

SA: Hmm. Takes good pictures too. In fact, you can store up to 5,000 photos in its memory.

C: Really ...?

C
- Tell the students they will now hear three more introductions and they are to imagine the situation and language in the same way they did in 2A.
- Play recording 2.2, but stop the recording after each introduction in order to give students time to collect their ideas. Encourage them to use diagrams similar to the one you have just drawn on the board.

Support
- With less confident groups, get class feedback on ideas after they have heard the introduction, but before playing the dialogue. However, you should give them at least one or two unaided goes at this exercise.

2.2 **LISTENING SCRIPT**

1 You will hear a man enquiring about buying a computer.

2 You will hear a shop assistant talking to a customer about mobile phones.

3 You will hear a woman complaining about a faulty radio.

D
- Tell students they will hear dialogues for each of the situations they heard in C.
- Ask them to note if their predictions about the situations and language used were correct.
- Play the recording, pausing after each dialogue to give students time to discuss their predictions with a partner.
- Finally, elicit feedback from the class about their predictions. Ask *Which words in the introduction made it easy to predict the content?*

2.3 **LISTENING SCRIPT**

1

(C = Customer; SA = Shop assistant)

SA: Good morning, sir. Can I help you?

C: Yes, I'm looking for a computer.

SA: Desktop, laptop or palmtop?

C: I'm not sure. A desktop, I think.

SA: All our desktops are over here. Now what kind of thing do you want to use it for?

C: Writing documents, mainly. My old one has just died!

SA: Well, I'm sure we can find you a replacement. And do you need a monitor as well?

2

(C = Customer; SA = Shop assistant)

SA: Good afternoon.

C: Hello. I was looking at your mobile phones ...

SA: Did you see anything you like? This one here is very popular. It has a full colour screen, a built-in camera and polyphonic ringtones.

C: Does it have video messaging?

SA: No. I'm sorry. Text and picture messaging only.

C: And which networks can I use it on?

3

(C = Customer; SA = Shop assistant)

SA: Yes, Madam? Can I help you?

C: I hope so. It's this radio. I bought it here a few weeks ago and it's stopped working.

SA: Oh dear! So what is the problem exactly?

C: Well, it's the volume control. It just doesn't work. No matter how much you turn it, it just doesn't get any louder.

SA: Hmm ... Could be the batteries.

C: No. I tried that. Still no good.

SA: OK. We'll let our workshops take a look at it. Now can I take down some details. Er, your name, please?

Extension: *Continuing the dialogue*

Aim: *To provide further practice with the vocabulary and expressions introduced in this unit, by having students write and perform short scripts.*

▸ Ask students how they think dialogue 2.2, in which a customer is enquiring about buying a camera, may develop.

▸ Elicit from the students any topic related words or functional language that might be used.

▸ Write the following extension to the dialogue on the board.

SA: *If you like, you can transfer your pictures onto a computer.*

C: *And can I print from the camera?*

SA: *Not directly, no. However, we do have a model which does just that. It is a little more expensive though.*

C: *May I see it?*

SA: *Of course ...*

▸ Put the students into pairs. Ask each pair to choose another situation from 2 and to extend the dialogue by writing a few more lines of speech.

▸ During the task, circulate and monitor, correcting and supplying language as needed.

▸ Finally, ask willing pairs of students to perform their dialogue extensions for the class. Invite other students to guess which situation they have chosen.

---

3 Identifying the question

Aim: To highlight the importance of, and give students practice in identifying the question they are being asked, a particularly important skill in task types where the question is not explicit, such as notes completion and form completion.

Go through the introductory information that begins this set of exercises. Ask the students to follow in their books as you read.

A
▸ Ask the students to complete the notes in the left hand column so that they are true for them.

▸ Remind students to use no more than three words and/or a number for each answer.

▸ Point out that note 2 requires a day or a date, but not a place.

▸ When they have finished, you may like to ask one or two students to read out their answers, and correct any errors.

B
▸ Explain that each statement in the first column is the answer to a question in the middle column. Use the example for statement 3, where the question is *How old are you?*

▸ Ask students to write the questions for the three remaining statements.

▸ Check the answers as a class, possibly writing them on the board. When checking the answers, point out there may be more than one possibility, e.g. *When were you born?/What is your date of birth?*

ANSWER KEY

1 What is your name?

2 When were you born?/What is your date of birth?

3 How old are you?

4 Why are you taking IELTS?/Why do you want to take IELTS?

Express tip

Read out the advice in this box while students follow in their books. Tell them that one of the problems students have with listening exercises is that they become confused and anxious about words and phrases they don't understand. Often, if they use their common sense, they can work out what these unknown words may mean. They just need to keep calm and keep thinking!

C
▸ Put the students into pairs. Ask each pair to practise asking and answering the questions in the table above. Have them complete the notes in their books with information about their partner.

▸ When they have finished, you could ask them to report their findings to the class (if in a smallish group) or to a new partner. Ask the students to use the information from the right hand column, but with the structures in the left hand column. E.g. *Her name is Tomoko. She was born on February 12*[th] *1984 ...*

4 Identifying the answer type

Aims: To highlight the importance of, and provide practice in identifying the type of answer being listened for.

To give students initial exposure to an IELTS notes completion listening task type.

A
▸ Direct students' attention to the notes and explain that the first column contains examples of questions found in IELTS notes completion tasks.
▸ Have students discuss in pairs what they think the topic of conversation will be. When they have finished, elicit the following suggestions from the class: a mobile phone (sending a text; network; top-up card; hands free), which will be given as a present.

B
▸ Tell students that they must identify the question being asked. Ask them to work individually and read the gapped notes in the first column and then choose the correct question word from the box.
▸ Tell students to write this question word in the correct space in the middle column. The first one has been done as an example.
▸ Check answers first in pairs, then as a class.

ANSWER KEY

1 who?	5 where?
2 how much?	6 how many?
3 which?	7 what percentage?
4 when?	8 why?

C
▸ Tell the students that this time they must identify the type of answer required. Ask them to work individually and read the gapped notes in the first column again and then choose the correct answer type from the box.
▸ Tell the students to write the type of answer in the column on the right. The first one has been done as an example.
▸ Check answers, first in pairs, then as a class.

ANSWER KEY

1 name	5 place
2 amount (of money)	6 number
3 name	7 percentage
4 time	8 reason

D
▸ Tell students they will now hear the dialogue which accompanies this set of notes.
▸ Ask them to listen and answer questions 1–8.
▸ Play recording 2.4.
▸ After listening, have students check their answers with a partner. Then elicit answers from the class and check together.
▸ Remind students they can read the listening script for this task at the back of the Coursebook.
▸ Ask the students to close their books, sit back and relax and listen to the dialogue again.

Support
▸ If students find this activity difficult, stop the recording after each answer and check as a class before moving on.

ANSWER KEY

1 George	5 newsagents and supermarkets
2 10/ten cents	6 120
3 ABC	7 87%
4 (in the) evening(s)	8 (much) safer

Challenge
▸ If your students have mobile phones, ask them about their particular mobile or network, to get the same information that is in the listening exercise.

2.4 **LISTENING SCRIPT** ───────────

(C = Customer; SA = Shop assistant)

SA: Good afternoon.

C: Hello. I'm looking for a mobile phone.

SA: OK. Well, you've come to the right place. Did you want any particular model?

C: Well, it's a birthday present for <u>my son, George</u>.

SA: OK. And how old is he?

C: George? He's 13 next week.

SA: Ah! A teenager! Is this his first phone?

C: Yes. We want to be able to contact him when he's out and he wants to chat with his friends.

SA: Well, this phone is very good for texting, you know, sending SMS messages. It's got predictive text and all that. That's what all the teenagers want. They're text mad!

C: Really?! Is it expensive to send a text?

SA: Not as much as making calls. On this particular network, it only <u>costs 10 cents</u>.

C: 10 cents! That's pretty cheap.

SA: Yeah. Some networks are even cheaper.

C: Such as?

SA: Let me see ... At the moment <u>the cheapest network is ABC</u>.

C: ABC.

SA: Yeah. But, as with all networks, it depends what time you use it.

C: Oh really?

SA: On this network, the most expensive time is morning. But if you call <u>in the evenings, you can save the most</u>.

C: OK. I'll tell him that. By the way, how does he pay for the calls?

SA: Two ways. Contract, but he'd need a bank account for that. For teenagers its best to have 'Pay As You Go'. This way you pay in advance for all your calls and you never get any nasty bills. You just have to buy a top-up card now and again.

C: Where can you buy those?

SA: Top-up cards? <u>Most newsagents and supermarkets sell them</u> these days.

C: Good. What about abroad?

SA: Sorry?

C: My son is going abroad on a school trip. They are going on a Mediterranean cruise. And they'll be stopping at lots of different countries. Can he use it in Europe?

SA: Sure. He can use it and buy top-up cards in <u>120 countries worldwide</u>.

C: Fantastic! One last thing. We often go cycling in the mountains. What's the coverage like?

SA: It depends. This network is quite good. They say it covers <u>87% of the country,</u> which isn't bad.

C: Ok. I'll take it.

SA: Fine. Now, will you be needing a hands-free kit?

C: A what?

SA: A hands-free kit. It allows you to use the phone without using your hands. Basically, if he does a lot of cycling, it's much safer to be in control of your bicycle. This way he can make calls and still be in control. <u>It's much safer</u>.

C: OK. I'll have that too. Now how much is it?

5 Form completion

Aims: To introduce form completion questions as a task type.

To give students the opportunity to consolidate the skills introduced in this section.

For this task

▸ Ask students to close their books.

▸ Tell them that they are about to do an exam-style form completion task. Explain that in the exam they are given time to read through the questions. Ask them what they would do in this time. If necessary, refer them to the *For this task* box.

▸ Write the following steps on the board.
Read the instructions and questions. Take note of how many words you can use.

Imagine the situation. Think about what type of language you will hear.

Identify the question.

Identify the answer type.

▸ Tell students they will hear a man buying a computer and that they have to complete the form. Ask them to work through the pre-listening stages as outlined above. Don't worry about timing at this stage, the important thing is that they practise the preparatory procedure.

▸ Exam practice recordings should be played through in their entirety without pausing. Before you start the recording, give your students some time to read through the questions, but tell them that this will not happen in the exam.

▸ Play recording 2.5 without stopping – it shows the students just how much preparation time they will have in the real exam. In the actual exam, where there is more than one task type, students are given more reading time (about 20 seconds) between task types.

▸ Let students check their answers with a partner before checking as a class. If students have difficulty with any of the questions, have them find the answers in the listening script at the back of the Coursebook.

▸ Ask them to close their books and play the recording one more time.

Support

▸ Play the recording again if necessary, but remind students it is only played once in the exam.

Express tip

Read out the advice in this box while students follow in their books. Stress once again that in the Listening and Speaking Sections of the exam, answers will be marked as incorrect if they are spelled incorrectly.

2.5 LISTENING SCRIPT ────────────

(C = Customer; SA = Shop assistant)

SA: Now, sir. Have you thought about caring for your new computer?

C: Sorry?

SA: By taking out an extended warranty on your new computer, you don't have to worry about it breaking down.

C: That sounds good. Is it expensive?

SA: If you take it out at the same time as you buy your computer, we'll give you a 25% discount, which works out at £15 a month.

C: Sounds good. I'll take it.

SA: OK, let me just get the form. Now, sir. I need to get a few personal details. Could I have your name, please?

C: It's Banks. Jonathan Banks.

SA: Could you spell that for me, please?

C: Yes. It's Jonathan, J-O-N-A-T-H-A-N, Banks, B-A-N-K-S.

SA: Thank you. And that's Mr.

C: Doctor, actually.

SA: Really? Do you know, I've been having terrible pains in my lower back, I ...

C: I'm sorry. I'm not that sort of doctor ...

SA: Oh!

C: I'm a doctor of Philosophy.

SA: Oh, right, Philosophy ... Address?

C: 17A, Leigham Street, Newtown.

SA: 70 or 17?

C: 17. 17A, Leigham Street.

SA: Can you spell that for me, please?

C: Yes. It's L-E-I-G-H-A-M.

SA: Ok. And do you know your postcode?

C: It's NT3 50P.

SA: N-T-3, 5-O-P. And do have a telephone number? Preferably a daytime number.

C: It's 01382 25669.

SA: Erhuh ... And what about an e-mail address. I presume you'll be keeping the same one.

C: Yes, It's banks123@fastnet.com

SA: OK ... fine. One last thing. Do you want us to put your name on our mailing list to keep you informed of any new products or special offers?

C: I don't think so. No. No, thank you.

SA: OK ... How would you like to pay – cash, cheque, credit card or hire purchase?

C: Here's my card ...

Extension: *Form completion practice*

Aim: *To provide further practice in completing forms by using authentic forms.*

Preparation

▸ You will need examples of forms in English, taken, as far as possible, from authentic sources. These forms could be application forms, contest entry forms cut from the newspaper, or forms printed off websites. If you have no access to forms, you could make them yourself.

▸ Make one copy of each form for each student. If you want them to work with more than one student, make more copies.

Procedure

▸ Put the students into pairs. Give one copy of each form to each student, so that all students have their own form(s).

▸ Have students interview their partner and fill in their form with their partner's details.

▸ For further practice, have students change partners and repeat the activity.

---

6 Notes completion

Aims: To provide practice with a notes completion task.

To give students the opportunity to further consolidate the skills introduced in this section.

Exam practice

▸ Tell the students that they are going to do an exam-style notes completion task. Remind them that in the exam they are given time to read through the questions. Ask them to tell their partners what they would do in this time. Again, they can check their answers with the *For this task* box.

▸ This time, don't give the students time to prepare before starting to play the recording. Remind the class that they will be given time to read the questions before they listen.

▸ Play recording 2.6 straight through.

▸ Afterwards, let students check their answers with each other, then find their answers in the listening script at the back of the Coursebook.

▸ Check the answers as a class.

▸ Ask them to close their books and play the recording one more time.

ANSWER KEY

1 green	6 a/one hundred/100
2 clock	7 Parker
3 four/4	8 (the) Olympic
4 39.99	9 solar power
5 TV	10 18

2.6 LISTENING SCRIPT

(C = Customer; SA = Shop assistant)

SA: Yes, madam. How can I help you?

C: I want to buy a radio. It's a present for my daughter.

SA: One moment, madam. I'll show you what models we have in stock.

C: Thank you.

SA: This one's very popular, 'The Club Tropicana'.

C: 'The Club Tropicana'! It's certainly very colourful, isn't it?

SA: The colours are very popular with children. It comes in pink, orange and green.

C: Oh, yes. I think she'd like that.

SA: And it's got a CD player and a clock.

C: Does the clock have an alarm? My daughter is terrible at getting up in the mornings.

SA: Yes, it does.

C: It's a bit big.

SA: That's because it has four built-in speakers, madam.

C: How much is it?

SA: Well, it usually retails at $59.99, but it's on special offer this week, so I could let you have it for 39.99.

C: $39.99. Uhm. Not bad. Anything else?

SA: There certainly is. Introducing our top of the range model: 'The Night Owl'. Available only in black. But packed with extra features.

C: Such as?

SA: A clock. And it has a television complete with 10 cm screen. And, and this makes it perfect for the bedside table, a built-in reading light.

C: Very clever!

SA: Yes. It's ideal for use both indoors and out. The batteries last for 100 hours.

C: Sounds good. Who's it made by?

SA: Parker, madam. They're a British company. Very good quality.

C: Parker ... How much is this one?

SA: $79.99, plus tax.

C: That's a bit expensive. Do you have anything cheaper?

SA: Here. This is the cheapest, smallest and lightest one we do.

C: It's tiny! And it's round! That's really unusual.

SA: Yep. It's called 'The Olympic'. You wear it round your neck with this special strap. See?

C: Oh! It's like a medal! An Olympic medal!

SA: That's why it's gold. And you get a free pair of headphones so you can listen to it wherever you are! And you never have to replace the batteries!

C: Really? Why not?

SA: There aren't any!

C: Oh?

SA: It runs on solar power.

C: Does it really? And I suppose it's expensive?

SA: $18, madam.

C: I'll take it.

SA: Certainly, madam. Now, cash, cheque or credit card?

Note:
▸ If your students are preparing for the General Training Module, they should turn to GT1A on page 72.

Section aims:
▸ To introduce the skills required to describe bar charts, pie charts and tables, by interpreting general and specific information, and comparing and contrasting data.
▸ To provide instruction on structuring a chart description essay correctly, i.e. moving from an overview of the chart to looking at specific details.
▸ To introduce and provide practice with Academic Writing Task 1.

1 Introduction

Aims: To introduce the topic of shopping through the Internet.

To provide a lead-in to the information being presented in the bar chart in the following section.

In the exam

▸ Draw students' attention to the information in the *In the exam* box outlining the Academic Writing Task 1.

▸ Clarify what bar charts, pie charts and tables are, by drawing examples on the board.

▸ Make sure students are aware of what a formal style consists of. Write the phrases below on the board – you will need to mix them up – and ask the students to decide if each one uses a formal academic style or informal spoken style. Then ask students to match the formal phrase with its informal equivalent.

we should also look at ...	*another thing to note is ...*
The numbers do not change.	*The numbers don't change.*
3 times as many as	*lots more than*
a great deal of	*lots and lots*
a relatively small percentage	*not very much*

2 Understanding charts and tables

Aims: To make students aware of the importance of spending some time studying the chart so that they are clear what information is being presented.

To familiarise students who haven't had much experience with this kind of data with the conventions of charts and graphs.

To show how information can be represented in different formats – in this case, both a bar chart and a table.

A ▸ Put students into pairs to discuss questions 1–4. Stress that the time the students spend thinking about the chart before they write will save them time when they begin writing and help them write more accurately.

ANSWER KEY

Suggested answers

1 The title gives us an overview of the contents of the graph. It is very useful in helping to write a first sentence, although you should point out to students that it is unwise to simply copy the opening sentence of the question, as they will get no credit for it.

2 The vertical axis tells us what percentage of people use the Internet and shop online.

3 The horizontal axis gives us a breakdown of the different age groups surveyed.

4 The colour key tells us something about the respondents; in this case, it differentiates between those using the Internet and those using it to shop.

B ▸ Have students transfer the information from the chart to the table.
▸ Check answers as a class.

ANSWER KEY

1 65%;	2 20%;	3 5%

Express tip

Read out the advice in this box while students follow in their books. Point out in the *express tip* that the mark allocation is not the same for Task 1 and Task 2. This is also reflected in the minimum word count (Task 1 requires a minimum of 150 words, and Task 2 requires a minimum of 250 words). Students should therefore spend only 20 minutes on Task 1 and be quite strict with themselves over this time limit.

3 Describing general and specific information

Aims: To provide students with a structure upon which they can base their descriptions of the visual data.

To help students know which information in a bar chart to focus on and describe.

A ▸ Have students use the chart in 2A to build a description using sections a–f. The exercise is designed to allow students to discover the pattern used in building such descriptions.

▸ Write the phrases below on the board to help students build up a bank of expressions. You should refer to the language bank on the back cover flap of the Coursebook for alternative ways of introducing these different kinds of sentences.

The chart shows …

One of the first things to note is that …

For example …

Another thing which stands out in this chart is that …

For instance …

A final point to note is that …

More specifically …

Support

▸ If you think your class needs support doing this activity, point out that each time an overall trend is described, it is followed by specific detail to illustrate the trend. You may choose to tell your students this either before or after they do the exercise, depending on their level and how difficult they might find the task.

Express tip

Read out the advice in this box while students follow in their books. Point out that any interpretation of the reasons for the data in these type of tasks will not gain marks and is therefore a waste of valuable time.

B ▸ Use this exercise to clarify whether sentences are overview statements, describe overall trends or describe specific detail.

▸ Read the instructions here to the class and check that students are clear on the difference between overview statements, overall trends and specific details.

▸ Have students work in pairs to categorise the five sentences.

▸ Check answers as a class.

4 Comparing and contrasting data

Aims: To provide revision of simple comparative language structures, and give practice making comparisons with the data.

To introduce the idea of pie charts as an alternative way of presenting data.

A ▸ Have students choose the appropriate words to produce correct sentences. Note that in some of the sentences there is more than one correct answer – e.g. *although* and *while* are both correct in **1**.

B ▸ Introduce a class discussion on what kind of online purchases students in your class make. How often do they spend money online? What kind of things do they spend money on?

▸ Have students work with a partner to look at the chart and discuss it. What can they see? What features stand out?

▸ Have students choose the appropriate words to produce correct sentences. These sentences in A and B can be referred to when students are writing the description later in the unit.

C ▸ Ask students to produce their own sentences describing both the bar chart and the pie chart. They should write some sentences with factual errors (you should monitor closely at this stage and correct any grammatical mistakes which may confuse the activity). You could get the ball rolling with one or two sentences on the board, e.g.
Nearly twice as many 18–24 year olds use the Internet as 55 year olds and over.

*More older people use the Internet than younger
people.*

▸ Put the students into pairs. Ask them to show their
sentences to their partner who will to decide if they
are correct or not. They should provide a corrected
version accordingly.

▸ When each pair has finished, have students change
partners and repeat.

Extension: *Making a quiz*

Aim: *To revise comparative structures by having students
prepare and administer a quiz.*

Procedure

▸ Put the students into pairs or small groups of 3–5
students. Each group will prepare a quiz on paper, and
ask their questions to another group.

▸ Tell the students to write a quiz consisting of ten true
or false questions using comparatives, e.g.
A horse is bigger than a donkey;

*There are more people living in Rio de Janeiro than
Buenos Aires;*

The Pacific Ocean is not as big as the Atlantic Ocean,
etc.

If you have access to the Internet, you can allow
students time to research their facts.

▸ When each pair or group has finished writing their quiz,
have them ask their questions to another group.

▸ For further practice, have each group ask their quiz to a
new group.

Extension: *Class survey*

Aim: *To give further practice in analysing, organising and
speaking about data, by using the results of a class
survey.*

Preparation

▸ If you are able to find examples of survey results from
newspapers or the Internet, make copies, bring them
into class and use them as examples of the kind of
surveys that students will be conducting in this
exercise.

Procedure

▸ Tell the students that they will carry out a survey and
collect data about the class. They will then present the
results to the rest of the class in a visual format. This
activity will take up quite a lot of class time, but if you
have the time, it will really help students to come to
grips with analysing and describing visual data.

▸ Present examples of surveys from the newspaper or
Internet to give students some ideas of things they
might carry out a survey on. This could be something
very simple like nationality or age range in the class, or
more complex, e.g. TV viewing habits or mobile phone
or Internet usage.

▸ Put the class into groups of 4–5 students. Have each
group choose a topic for their questionnaire. They
should then prepare questions to ask the whole class.
To save time, they should prepare a maximum of five
questions.

▸ When students have prepared their questions, they can
ask as many other students as possible. If you have a
small class, think about carrying out the survey on
another class.

▸ After each group has asked their questions, they should
collate the results and change the statistical
information into visual information. They need to
present their results in the form of a bar chart, pie
chart or table. For further practice, they could present
the same data in different formats or types of graph.

▸ Finally, have students prepare a mini-presentation
reporting their findings. Point out that they should only
pick out 2 or 3 main points to talk about. Encourage
them to make sentences comparing and contrasting the
data, as in the Coursebook, and support each
description with statistical data.

5 Academic Writing Task 1: Report

Aims: To give students the opportunity to consolidate the
skills introduced in this unit.

To practise a complete Academic Writing Task 1.

To practise writing within a specified time limit.

For this task

▸ Read through the *For this task* box and have students
follow. The areas covered in the unit are recapped
here, but emphasise that students should spend time
studying the chart before they start writing. It is very

tempting for students to start writing before they have a clear idea of what they are writing about.

▶ Have students work through the various stages in pairs, i.e. studying the chart in detail, deciding what the main features are, applying language to pick out the main points and details, working out one or two sentences where they can make a comparison. They should make notes as they do this.

Exam practice

▶ The actual writing can be set as homework or done in class. After students have done all the preparation, you could allow them 20 minutes writing time. Students will probably find this time limit very short, but point out that in the exam they have to do the preparation and the writing in 20 minutes. Any subsequent practice should allow 20 minutes for preparation and writing.

▶ When marking the work, look for the following:
  - An introductory sentence which uses the title, axes and key to inform the reader of what is being described.
  - A second sentence which says something very general about the chart, e.g. 'the purchases vary widely between both countries and type of purchase'.
  - About 3 further major features of the graph which are supported by statistical evidence.

▶ You should use the following criteria to assess the writing:
  - task fulfilment (does the student describe the graph well?)
  - coherence and cohesion (is it logically organised and linked together clearly?)
  - vocabulary and sentence structure.

Model answer

The chart shows a range of goods and services bought last year by Internet shoppers in three different countries, namely Australia, Canada and the UK. We can see that the percentage of consumers making such purchases varied widely according to product/service and country.

One of the first things to note is that, generally speaking, a higher percentage of consumers in the UK made online purchases than in the other countries, with the exception of toys and financial services. More specifically, Internet book sales in the UK exceeded those in Australia and Canada by almost a third. A similar comparison of music sales showed UK purchases to be almost double those of other countries.

Another thing which stands out is that in all countries, purchases of certain products were much higher than others. For example, in the UK, 64% of consumers bought music online, compared with only 2% for financial services. On the whole, sales of entertainment goods and computer equipment were much higher than other goods and services. These sales were roughly two to three times higher than goods such as food/drink and toys.

Jobs and Job-hunting

Section aims:
▸ To look in more detail at paraphrase and, in particular, matching keywords in the question to paraphrased information in the text.
▸ To practise a number of task types – table completion; sentence completion and matching information to sections of text.

1 Introduction

Aim: To introduce the topics of jobs and job-hunting and some of the job-related vocabulary which arises later in the unit.

A ▸ Put the students into pairs and have them discuss the questions with their partner.

▸ Elicit from the class a list of the jobs they discussed and write them on the board. Use this list of jobs to generate vocabulary by asking for words associated with each job. For example, **bus driver:** *bus, drive, tickets, route, uniform, vehicle;* **architect:** *plans, draw, building, blueprints, design;* **doctor:** *hospital, patients, white coat, stethoscope, medicine, prescription.*

B ▸ Demonstrate the activity first, by having one student choose one of the jobs written on the board without telling you which one it is. Ask that student 'yes/no' questions to guess what the job is. E.g. *Do you wear a uniform? Do you work outside? Do you earn a lot of money? Do you operate a machine? Do you work in the evenings?* etc.

▸ Have students work with a partner or in small groups to carry out the activity for themselves.

Support

▸ This activity can be made less difficult by having students use the list of jobs on the board as a limited pool of words from which they can choose.

In the exam

▸ Have the students read the information in the *In the exam* box. Use the information to explain about matching tasks. Explain that in the Academic Training module, the format of the text is different to that of the General Training module – paragraphed text is used rather than advertisements – but that the skills and tasks are the same.

2 Identifying keywords and paraphrase

Aims: To encourage students to use pictures to generate vocabulary, and in particular, to think of different ways to describe the same thing, i.e. synonym and paraphrase.

To practise identifying keywords within a text.

A ▸ Elicit from the class job titles for the pictures at the top of page 24. You could include: *news reporter, TV journalist, correspondent, member of the press, scientist, chemist, researcher,* etc.

▸ For each of the jobs chosen above, elicit a list of responsibilities that each occupation has. E.g. *The window cleaner cleans windows, polishes glass, works high off the ground,* etc. Encourage students to use a range of different expressions to describe the jobs. Establish the idea that there are many ways of saying the same thing.

▸ Students should skim the advertisement on page 25 and match it to the correct picture.

ANSWER KEY

The advertisement matches the picture of the TV journalist.

B ▸ Ask students to read the advertisement carefully. Have them underline the keywords that identify the job being advertised.

ANSWER KEY

Keywords include: news channel, journalist, covering events, journalism.

C ▸ Have students search the text for synonyms and paraphrase in this controlled matching activity.

Extension: *Building up from keywords*

Aim: To build awareness of keywords within a text, using authentic magazine and newspaper articles.

Preparation

▸ Choose 10 sentences taken from newspapers and magazines, for example, *In the United States, company workers are expected to work hard, in fact, their vacations last year were, on average, only 5.4 days.* Write 5 of them on one sheet of paper and 5 on another.

▸ Make one copy of each sheet for each pair of students, so that each student in the pair has a different list of sentences.

Procedure

▸ Write keywords from your example sentence on the board, *United States / work hard / vacation / average / 5.4 days*, and have students try to write a sentence from the keywords.

▸ Emphasise that it is not important whether students are able to recreate the sentence exactly, it is more important that they are building up their awareness of keywords within a text.

▸ Put the students into pairs. Give each student a list of sentences, ensuring that each student in a pair has a different list.

▸ Have students take turns identifying the keywords from one of their sentences and giving them to their partner, without showing the original sentence. The partner will then try to create a sentence from the keywords.

3 Matching information to sections of text

Aim: To introduce matching information to sections of text as a task type.

For this task
Exam practice Questions 1–4

▸ Read through the *For this task* box, pointing out that the answers are based on paraphrased information.

▸ Ask students to focus on the pictures and think of different ways of describing them, then scan the advertisements to find the job title which matches the pictures.

Exam practice Questions 5–10

▸ Have students pick out keywords in the question sentences 5–10.

▸ Ask students to read the advertisements to look for paraphrased information.

Support

▸ If your class has difficulty with the text, pre-teach the following vocabulary:
patient; apply/application form; immediate; straightaway

▸ Test their understanding of the vocabulary through 'odd one out' questions, e.g.
education/learning/training/working (*working* is the 'odd one out', or *ill/nurse/patient/healthy* (*healthy* is the 'odd one out').

4 Table completion

Aims: To introduce table completion questions as a task type.

To give students the opportunity to consolidate the skills introduced in this section.

For this task
▸ Have students read the information in the *For this task* box. Point out that it is important to take a few seconds to study the whole table before they begin searching for an answer. Remind them exactly what they should be paying attention to when they study the table, e.g. row and column headings. Note that the order of the questions and the information in the text is the same.

Exam practice
▸ Have students complete the task by looking in the relevant part of the text, in this case, the correct job advertisement. As with many of the task types, many of the answers are based on paraphrased information.
▸ Check answers as a class.

ANSWER KEY

11 Yes

12 275

13 (call) in person

14 16, 525

15 email

Express tip
Read out the advice in this box while students follow in their books. Demonstrate this information by pointing out that the order of jobs down the left side of the table is the same as the order of jobs in the four advertisements. Also, within each row of the table, the information follows the order in which it is found in each ad, i.e. 'Pay' details are listed above 'Experience' information, which is listed above 'Application' details.

5 Sentence completion

Aims: To introduce sentence completion questions as a task type.

To give students the opportunity to further consolidate the skills introduced in this section.

For this task
▸ Generate interest in the topic by asking students what someone can do to find a job.
▸ Tell students that they are going to read a text about job-hunting.
▸ Go through the task rubric in the *For this task* box, making sure that students predict answers before they read, but are also aware that more than one sentence

---

ending may seem to fit as a correct answer, and it is therefore important not to rely on common sense, but to read the text for the answer.
▸ Point out that, as in the previous task, the questions appear in the same order as the relevant information in the task.

Exam practice
▸ Have students skim the text, looking for the relevant part. When they find this section of the text, they should read more carefully, looking for synonyms and paraphrasing.

ANSWER KEY

Questions 1–4

1 Answer: better-informed decision
Note 'Finding out as much as possible will help you make a better informed decision.'

2 Answer: a good salary
Note 'Don't just apply for a job because it has a good salary.'

3 Answer: voluntary work
Note 'Think of the skills and qualifications you need to get that first valuable job and how you might go about getting them. ... there may be other, less immediately obvious, routes, such as doing voluntary work.'

4 Answer: a job advertisement
Note 'A great many jobs are found without responding to a job advertisement at all.'

Questions 5–8

5 Answer: E
Note '... a careers office or library ... you should take advantage of them, ...'

6 Answer: C
Note ' ... and help you decide what job will suit you.'

7 Answer: A
Note 'To open the door to a wider variety of jobs ...'

8 Answer: H
Note 'What are you good at? What are you interested in?'

SPEAKING

1 Introduction

Aims: To show students that speaking for a extended period is not as difficult as it might first appear, as this is something which they do everyday.

To provide a first attempt at speaking, using a typical Part 2 Topic card.

A ▸ Ask students which of the situations they have been in.

▸ Have them talk in pairs or small groups to compare their experiences.

▸ Give feedback to the whole group, making the point that talking for a long time does not have to be in a formal situation, and in fact, everyone does it almost every day.

B ▸ Have students discuss what ideas they might include when talking about the card. You could share one or two ideas with the class before students then go on to talk about the card with their partner. Make sure students are clear that they have to speak for a period of time without interrupting each other.

C ▸ Have students discuss in small groups or as a class what they found difficult about the task. Elicit feedback from students.

▸ Note: Students will probably have problems doing the task. They are likely to say that they did not have enough to say, weren't sure what was expected of them, or that they felt too nervous to speak. You should explain that in the actual exam task, they will have 1 minute to prepare how to speak and that they will look at how best to use this time in order to generate ideas and organise what they want to say. If they feel confident about what they are going to say, they will feel less nervous.

Extension: *Just a minute*

Aim: *To provide further speaking practice by having students speak for one minute without stopping.*

Preparation

▸ Think of 12 topics for students to talk about, for example, *My last birthday*, or *What I love about holidays, My favourite meal*, etc and write them on a sheet of paper so they look like cards. Photocopy and cut them up so that each group of students has a set of 12 'cards'.

Procedure

▸ Put the students into groups of 3 or 4 and put a set of Topic cards face down in the centre of each group.

▸ Each student in the group takes it in turn to take a card and speak on that topic for one minute without stopping. You can give bonus points for good vocabulary or high level of fluency, etc – roughly follow the criteria set for this part of the exam.

▸ Allow a few questions at the end of the minute from other students.

▸ Repeat until each member of the group has had at least two opportunities to speak.

In the exam

Draw students' attention to the *In the exam* box. As students will probably feel nervous about this speaking task, emphasise the fact that they will have the opportunity to prepare notes to help them.

2 Checking you understand the topic card

Aim: To introduce and practise an effective way in which students can ask for clarification of the information on the topic card if they do not understand it.

A ▸ Go through the information on the card, explaining how asking for clarification can actually impress the examiner.

▸ Point out the notes the student has made and the example question underneath the card. Direct students to the language box underneath. You could model some of the new language by asking for clarification of the word 'exactly' using different examples from the box.

B ▸ Treat this exercise as a controlled practice exercise.
▸ Have students ask for clarification of the other notes the student has made. Encourage them to use a variety of language from the box. There are more language points than notes on the card, but tell students it is OK to ask about the same point twice using different language, as the aim is to practise the language used to clarify the card.

3 Organising your ideas

Aim: To introduce the idea of making organised notes to help with extended speaking and provide an opportunity to practise this.

A ▸ Explain about the time allowed to make notes. Emphasise that 1 minute is a short time and that students should write notes including keywords – not full sentences.
▸ Have students read the notes, making sure they understand the vocabulary. Point out that the students have underlined the key vocabulary that they want to include. Students will get credit for their range of vocabulary, so point out that it's worth thinking of some 'higher level' (lower frequency) words as they make their notes, e.g. on notes B, the chef has underlined the word 'exhausted'.
▸ The cards are not in the same order as the speakers. Ask students to put the cards in the same order as they occur on the recording.

ANSWER KEY
Correct order of speakers is: C, A, B

3.1 **LISTENING SCRIPT**

1

Student 1: OK, let's see. The job I have at the moment is my first job. I am a waitress in a coffee bar. When I started, I only cleaned the tables. It was a little boring because I did the same thing all the time, but after a short time, I got a promotion – you know, a higher position. Now I make coffee and serve the customers at the cash register – it's more interesting. Would I do it in the future? I think, yes, why not? If I am a student, it is a good job to earn some money. The hours are very flexible – it is convenient in that way. What did I like? Hmmm ... Well, my colleagues are very nice, and so is my boss – they are very friendly. But what I really don't like is the uniform – it is a little stupid with this hat.

2

Student 2: Before I came back to my studies, I was a teacher in a primary school. My students were young – perhaps 5 or 6 years old. I taught students many many different subjects, for example, we studied reading and writing, and mathematics – errr, art and music, and others – but music was my favourite. I was a little like a mother in some ways – I listened to their problems sometimes. I enjoyed my job very much but now I want to change, I want to do something completely different in the future – but I'm not sure what exactly. I liked teaching very much – especially because I love children. But I did not like the administration. There were a lot of papers to write out everyday, and I'm not very good at office work.

3

Student 3: I used to be a chef in a kitchen in a busy restaurant. The restaurant was in a hotel and sometimes I cooked for 40 people, errr, guests in the hotel. I liked my job and would like to do it in the future, but especially if I could have my own restaurant. I liked it because it was creative and you could use your imagination, but the thing that I didn't like was it was very hard work. When I finished my work, I was usually exhausted. I was only able to go home and sleep ...

Express tip

Read out the advice in this box while students follow in their books. Explain that the examiner doesn't mark the student on the page of notes that they take, and doesn't even need to see them – they are only used to help the student speak.

B
▸ Play the recording again. As students listen, they should cross off the points they hear. Ask students which points were not mentioned by the students.
▸ Have students also pay attention to the underlined keywords and check that the speakers use them.

ANSWER KEY

A Teacher: The student didn't talk about 'piano'.
B Chef: The student didn't talk about 'wedding parties'.
C Waitress: The student didn't talk about '3 months'.

C
▸ Have students talk about the same card again. This time, they should make notes and consequently, find the task easier. You should allow quite a long time for this, enabling students to find keywords and respond to each point – it is more important at this stage that students prepare a good set of notes from which they can speak, rather than make the notes in a short time and then do poorly on the task. Monitor to ensure students make notes and don't write full sentences.

D
▸ Have students practise speaking about the card again with a different partner. They can, in fact, swap partners more than once. Students will inevitably feel more relaxed and perform better the more times they do the task.

4 Individual long turn

Aims: To provide students with the opportunity to speak in a relaxed exam type situation.

To practise Part 2 of the Speaking exam.

▸ Go through the *For this task* box, which recaps the main points of the section.
▸ Put students into pairs – candidate and examiner. Students should speak and listen for 1–2 minutes.

▸ Instruct the students who are 'examiners' that they will give feedback at the end and should therefore listen carefully.
▸ The 'examiners' should also ask one or two extra questions at the end to signal the time is up.

Support
▸ Have students pair up with another partner and repeat the activity. This will increase their confidence and fluency.

Express tip

Read out the advice in this box while students follow in their books. Remind them that keeping their finger on the card will stop them having to worry about losing their place while they look up from the card and make eye contact with the examiner while speaking.

IELTS Express Speaking Video

If you are using the *Speaking Video* which accompanies *IELTS Express*, Section 3 – Part 2 of the video relates to the content of this unit. The video could be shown at the beginning of this lesson to give students a general idea of the content and format of the Part 2 of the IELTS Speaking module. Alternatively, it could be shown at the end of the lesson to provide a recap and demonstration of the material covered in this unit.

For more information on the *IELTS Express Speaking Video* and how to integrate it into your lessons, see page 103.

4 Crime and Punishment

Section aims:

▸ To develop students' skills in using keywords to predict answers.

▸ To help students identify synonyms and paraphrasing.

▸ To introduce and to provide practice in Listening Section 2: Non-academic monologue and Section 3: Academic dialogue.

▸ To introduce and provide practice in multiple-choice questions; short-answer questions and notes completion tasks.

1 Introduction

Aims: To introduce the topic of crime and to introduce some of the vocabulary used later in this unit.

To introduce students to the types of conversation they will hear later in the unit, i.e. reporting a crime to the police.

A ▸ Ask one or two students to describe to the class what they can see in each picture. Ask what crime they think is being illustrated.

▸ Ask students to look at the crimes listed in the white box below the pictures. Read them out. Have students work in pairs and match each picture with a crime.

▸ Elicit answers, checking pronunciation. Ask for definitions of those four crimes which are not illustrated, again checking pronunciation.

▸ Ask students to work with their partner to make a list of any other crimes they know. Give them 2 or 3 minutes for this. If they like, they can use their dictionaries.

▸ When students have finished, ask for their ideas on other crimes. Write their answers on the board. Check the meaning and pronunciation and feed in other vocabulary you think would be useful. (See *Support* for ideas.)

ANSWER KEY

A murder; **B** smuggling; **C** arson; **D** burglary

Other crimes may include: blackmail, rape, mugging, forgery, treason, corruption*, etc

* Use your own judgement as to whether it would be insensitive to discuss certain crimes with your class.

Support

▸ Most students at this level would probably benefit from some support here. Introduce or check

understanding of some key topic vocabulary, which is also used later in this unit.

nouns (things): *crime, theft, valuable object, burglar alarm, description of someone/something*

nouns (people): *police, police officer, thief (thieves), burglar, witness, suspect, criminal*

verbs: *break into somewhere, steal something, to force open a window, arrest someone**

expressions: *to be in prison, to be worth a fortune, have make a positive ID, follow or have a lead*

(*This item is not used but is useful to know.)

B ▸ Tell the students that you have witnessed a crime and that you want to report it to the police. Tell them that they are the police and that they should ask you questions to find out information about the crime.

▸ Begin by saying *Hello, I want to report a crime.* Then prompt them to find out the details of the crime by eliciting questions. As they produce the questions, write them up on the board, giving answers as you go.

▸ Write some prompts up on the board:
Who ...? Where ...? What time ...? How old ... ? etc

ANSWER KEY

Police need information on:
time, place and nature of crime

description of suspects – height, weight, age, race, hair colour, clothing, distinguishing features (e.g. scars), etc

description of any vehicles involved, including make, model, age, colour, licence plate (registration number), etc.

Questions asked would need to elicit the above information.

In the exam

Before reading through this, ask students to close their books and tell each other what they know about Section 2 of the Listening exam. You could ask how it differs from Section 1 and how it is the same.

Then read the text in the *In the exam* box aloud and let students follow in their books.

2 Using keywords to predict the answer

Aims: To provide further practice in identifying keywords and using them to try to predict the answer.

To introduce students to short-answer questions and multiple-choice questions in the Listening exam.

A
▸ Ask students to imagine they are a businessman or businesswoman, whose briefcase has been stolen and that they are reporting the crime to the police. Ask what information the police would need and what questions they would be asked.

▸ Tell students they will hear a businesswoman reporting the theft of her briefcase. Direct them to look at question 1 in the white box. Tell them this is an example of a short-answer question.

▸ Ask students to identify, then underline or highlight the most important word or words in the question. Tell them that these keywords will help them find the answer. Throughout the course, insist on students underlining or highlighting keywords – this may seem unnecessary, but it is good discipline and training for the actual exam. Note: some examination centres will not allow students to use highlighters in the exam. It's probably best to check with the relevant centre on local exam procedures.

▸ As a class, discuss the questions beneath the white box.

▸ Play recording 4.1 while students listen and answer the question.

▸ Elicit and check answers.

> **ANSWER KEY**
> **Answer:** black
> keyword: colour
> answer required: a colour.
> The answer is more likely to be black or brown.

4.1 **LISTENING SCRIPT**

(PO = Police officer; BW = Businesswoman)

PO: Yes, madam?

BW: Hello. Good morning, officer. I'd like to report a crime. A theft. My briefcase has been stolen. <u>It's a black one</u>. It's really important I get it back.

B
▸ As a class, discuss the question in the white box.
▸ Play recording 4.2 while students listen and answer the question.
▸ Elicit and check answers.

> **ANSWER KEY**
> **Answer:** (a) (client) report
> keyword: papers
> The answer might be some sort of business papers: files, documents, reports, etc

4.2 **LISTENING SCRIPT**

(BW = Businesswoman)

BW: It's really important that I get it back. It had all sorts of things in it ... my mobile phone, some pens, a calculator. But the most important thing was some documents, <u>a report for a client</u>, the one I was going to meet. I must get that report back. It's extremely important.

C
▸ Remind students they were introduced to the idea of identifying the question in relation to form and notes completion in Unit 2. Here is another task type where this skill is required. Ask the students to identify the question.

▸ Explain that the first line of a multiple-choice question is called a question stem (like the stem of a plant) and that there are three options (A, B and C). Ask students to underline or highlight the keywords in the stem and each of the options.

▸ Check their answers. Ask them *Why is it important to underline 'dress' or 'dress shop' but not just 'shop'?*

▸ Tell students that sometimes it is possible to predict the answer to a question. Ask if any one option is more likely here. Tell them that even though all options are equally likely here, it is always a good idea to think what the answer might be before they listen.

▸ Play recording 4.3 while students listen and answer the question.

▸ Check the answers as a class.

Answer: A

The question being asked is 'Where was the briefcase stolen from?'

Two shops are mentioned in the question: a dress shop and a dry cleaner's shop. If students only choose 'shop' as the keyword, they may get the wrong answer.

All three answers are equally likely here.

4.3 LISTENING SCRIPT ——————

(PO = Police officer; BW = Businesswoman)

PO: Now where was this bag stolen from?

BW: Well ... I had lunch at a French restaurant with a friend ... but I still had it with me when I left. I was on the way to an important meeting with a client. But on the way, I had to drop off a dress at the dry cleaner's ... And that's when it happened, when I took the dress into the dry cleaner's. I left my briefcase <u>on the back seat of the car</u>. And when I came out, it was gone.

3 Identifying synonyms and paraphrase

Aims: To provide practice in identifying synonyms and paraphrasing.

To provide further practice in identifying keywords and answer types.

A ▸ Ask students to look at question 1 and identify the question being asked. Ask them to underline or highlight the keywords in the stem and in each of the options.

▸ Tell students that in the IELTS exam the words they hear in the Listening module may not be exactly the same as the words used in the question. Different words may be used to talk about the same thing, that is, the examiners may use synonyms or paraphrase.

▸ Ask students to work in pairs and to look again at the keywords they have identified and to try to think of any synonyms or paraphrases that they may hear in place of these keywords. Use option A as an example. Ask if there are other ways of saying '12:00'. Then ask them to consider alternative ways of expressing the remaining options.

▸ Elicit feedback on these alternatives.

▸ Play recording 4.4 while students listen and answer the question.

▸ Check answers in pairs and as a class.

Answer: C

The question being asked is 'What time did the theft occur?'

Ways of saying '12:00' include 'twelve o'clock', 'noon', 'midday' or even 'midnight'.

Ways of saying '1:45' include '(a) quarter to two', 'one forty-five', '(a) quarter to two' or '(a) quarter of two'.

Ways of saying '2:15' include 'two fifteen', '(a) quarter past two', '(a) quarter after two'.

4.4 LISTENING SCRIPT ——————

(BW = Businesswoman)

BW: What time was the theft? Now, let me see, what time was this? We met for lunch at one o'clock. And left the restaurant at two. The dry cleaner's is quite close to the restaurant, so it must have been <u>sometime around ten past two</u>.

Express tip

Read out the advice in this box while students follow in their books. Remind students of the work they have done on keywords, synonyms and paraphrase in previous units.

B ▸ Direct students to look at the example of the short-answer question in the white box and underline or highlight any keywords.

▸ Ask if they can think of any synonyms or paraphrases for 'vehicle'.

▸ Ask them to identify the answer type and try to predict the answer.

▸ Play recording 4.5 while students listen and answer the question.

▸ Check answer as a class.

Answer: (about) 5 minutes

keywords: away, her vehicle

synonyms: vehicle = car, van, motorbike, etc.

The type of answer is a time.

The answer is more likely to be a short time – minutes rather than hours.

4.5 LISTENING SCRIPT ——————

(BW = Businesswoman)

BW: I really don't understand how it could have happened. <u>Honestly, I only left the car for about five minutes ...</u>

C
- Ask students to look at question 3 and identify the question being asked. Ask them to underline or highlight the keywords in the stem and in each of the options.
- Ask students to work in pairs and to try to think of any synonyms or paraphrases for these keywords.
- Elicit feedback on these alternatives.
- Play recording 4.6 while students listen and answer the question.
- Check answers in pairs and as a class.

ANSWER KEY

Answer: A

The question being asked is 'Who does the woman suspect may have stolen her briefcase?'

keyword: who

synonyms: motorist = driver, someone driving a car
cyclist = a person on a bicycle
police officer = policeman, policewoman

4.6 LISTENING SCRIPT

(PO = Police officer; BW = Businesswoman)

BW: I don't know who could have taken it. The street was almost empty apart from one or two pedestrians. I did see a woman on a bicycle, but that was after I discovered the bag had gone. I do remember seeing a man sitting in a car parked opposite. He was just staring at me. And when I came out of the shop, he had gone. It must have been him. Really! These things wouldn't happen if we had more police officers on our streets.

PO: OK, madam. If I can just take down your name and address ...

Extension: *Script writing*

Aim: *To give students extra practice with vocabulary and functional language covered in the unit by having them write short dialogues.*

Procedure
- Put the students into pairs or small groups. Tell them that they are going to write their own short dialogue, similar to the one they have just heard, about somebody reporting a crime to the police. Explain that they can talk about something which actually happened to them or they can invent something, maybe based on one of the crimes shown or mentioned on the first page of this unit. Tell them to make use of the list of questions they made earlier in 1B.

- Set a time limit for writing of 10–15 minutes.
- Have students write their dialogues. As they work, circulate and monitor, correcting and feeding in new vocabulary where necessary.
- When they have finished, have students read out or perform their dialogues to the rest of the class.
- This exercise could also be set for homework.

4 Multiple-choice questions; short-answer questions

Aims: To give students the opportunity to consolidate skills introduced in this section.

To introduce multiple-choice questions as a task type.

To provide further practice with short-answer question tasks.

For this task
- Give your students a few minutes to read through the *For this task* box. Draw their attention to the last few points, which are new ideas.

Express tip
Read out the advice in this box while students follow in their books. This information applies to all IELTS Listening tasks, not just this one.

Exam practice Questions 1–5
- Play recording 4.7 and have students answer questions 1-5. For weaker groups, see *Support* below.

Support
- With less confident groups, work through the stages of the *For this task* box. First, look at questions 1–5. Help students to identify the keywords and any synonyms or paraphrasing, then play the recording.
- With very weak groups, you could stop the recording after each answer and elicit the answer from the students, playing it again if there are any problems.

4.7 **LISTENING SCRIPT**

(RA = Radio announcer; PO = Police officer)

RA: Coming up to 6:30 pm here on County FM. Time for our weekly 'County Crime Report'. Joining us now, our old friend Inspector Holland. Good evening to you, Inspector.

PO: Evening, Sue. Evening all. This week we'd like to ask listeners to help us with a particularly important crime – a burglary at <u>the County Museum</u> here in the centre of town. It involves the theft of several items of both local and national importance and despite having three of our most experienced officers on the case, we've very few leads so far.
What we do know is this. Sometime <u>on Saturday night or Sunday morning</u>, a gang of thieves broke in and stole several valuable objects. Firstly, an antique wall clock from the main gallery. Now, this clock is not only beautiful, it is also unique. In fact, it's the only surviving piece by the master clockmaker, George Mendelssohn. Consequently, <u>it is worth a small fortune</u>. In fact, it was last valued at £250,000.
The second item on the thieves' shopping list was a painting. A life-size portrait of local parliamentarian and anti-slave trade campaigner, Sir John Foxton. Now, those listeners who have visited the museum will almost certainly remember this painting. It's the very large painting of <u>the man on the white horse</u>. And for those of you who don't know it, this is a particularly fine painting by the renowned 19th century artist Henry Radley and is valued at around half a million pounds.
Now, how the burglars managed to get into the building is <u>a mystery</u>. No windows were broken. Nor was there any sign of any doors or windows being forced open. The burglar alarm failed to go off. Now, it's not impossible that they had a key – several people have keys to the side entrance.

Questions 6–10

▸ Play recording 4.8 and have students answer questions 6–10. For weaker groups, see *Support* below.

Support

▸ With less confident groups, work through the stages of the *For this task* box. First, look at questions 6–10. Help students to identify the keywords and any synonyms or paraphrasing, then play the recording.
▸ With very weak groups, you could stop the recording after each answer and elicit the answer from the students, playing it again if there are any problems.

Further Support

▸ After you've played the whole recording, ask students to turn to the back of the book and look at the listening script for recording 4.8.
▸ Ask the students to read the script. Then, working in pairs, ask them to look again at the questions and identify the keywords. Ask them to draw a circle round the answer (or in some questions, the information that leads them to the answer) and write the relevant question number. This will help them see the benefit of the keyword technique, as well as emphasising the importance of thinking about keywords. It should also demonstrate that they do not need to understand all of the dialogue in order to answer the questions; they need only understand the part containing the answer.
▸ Finally, ask students to close their books and play the recording through one last time.

4.8 LISTENING SCRIPT

(RA = Radio announcer; PO = Police officer)

PO: As I say, unfortunately, we have had few leads on this case. However, a witness who lives opposite the museum has been able to give us some information about who may have been involved. Now, this lady was woken up at around 3 am on the night in question by loud music directly outside her window. On looking out of her window, she saw a man sitting in the front of a van, shouting, singing. Now, this man is described as having a big white beard. The witness said he looked 'a bit like Father Christmas'. As for the van, no positive ID on the make, as yet. But the witness described it as blue or green. So, were you in the area of the museum late on Saturday night? Did you see *anything* suspicious? If so, please help us put these precious items back where they belong and these criminals in prison. If you have *any* information, please call the police now on the free hotline. That's 0800 666 000. 0800 666 000. That's it from me. Till the same time next week. Evening all.

RA: Our thanks to Inspector Holland there. You're listening to County FM. We'll be right back after this.

5 Multiple-choice questions; notes completion

Note: for more information on describing trends see Unit 6, Writing section.

Aims: To introduce students to a Section 3 Academic dialogue-style listening.

To provide further practice with multiple-choice and notes completion tasks.

▸ Ask students how they intend to approach these questions, i.e. what stages they will go through. If necessary, refer them to the *For this task* box on page 35. You may also ask them to read over the advice on notes completion tasks in Listening Unit 2 (page 19)

Exam practice Questions 1–4

▸ Play recording 4.9 and have students answer questions 1–4. For weaker groups, see *Support*.

ANSWER KEY	
1 A	3 C
2 B	4 A

Support

▸ On the board, create three columns, labelled: +, -, 0.

▸ Write the following items on the board: *a fall, a rise, to rise, no change, to decrease, an increase, a decrease, to go down, to drop, to go up, to increase, to stay the same.*

▸ Now ask students to put these items into the appropriate column.

▸ For more ideas refer to the *Further Support* section on page 40.

In the exam

▸ Ask students to close their books. Tell them they are about to hear an example of Section 3 of the Listening exam. Ask the following questions: *How many people will they hear speaking?* (2 or more)

Who are these people? (students, but sometimes also a tutor)

What kind of discussion will they hear? (an academic discussion)

▸ Now ask them to open their books, read the *In the exam* box and check their answers.

4.9 LISTENING SCRIPT

(D = Dave; A = Al)

D: Hi, Al!

A: Hi, Dave. Just working on our presentation for tomorrow. How's your bit coming along?

D: That's tomorrow? I thought it was next week.

A: You mean you've done nothing?

D: Look, Al, I've had a lot of things to do ...

A: OK. Don't worry. Sit down. This is what I think we should do. Firstly, let's give a few facts and figures about the crime rates here in London.

D: Like what?

A: Like in the last financial year, there were over one million crimes reported in the Greater London Area.

D: You're joking! Must have just been a bad year, right?

A: Well, it's an increase of almost 23,000 on the previous year, so I'm afraid it's a rising trend.

D: What sort of crimes? Murder?

A: Luckily, murder only accounted for a small percentage – under two hundred in total.

D: What about robberies?

A: Robberies totalled about 43,000.

D: 43,000! That an increase too?

A: <u>No, the previous year was almost 9,000 more</u>.

D: At least something's moving in the right direction. What about burglaries?

A: From homes or business premises?

D: Both.

A: Er ... let me see. <u>About the same year before – 113,000</u>. But that's not including shoplifting.

D: What about cars? There must be loads of car crime.

A: Yeah, half a million vehicles are stolen in the UK every year. In fact, vehicle crime accounts for about <u>25% of all reported crime</u>. That includes thieves stealing things from cars too.

D: So, what do you want me to do?

A: Perhaps you could give the audience some details and then maybe some advice about how to prevent car crime.

D: OK. Look, I'll do some research and meet you after lunch.

Exam practice Questions 5–10

▸ Play recording 4.10 and have students answer questions 5–10.

A: Yeah, I've been in some pretty scary car parks in my time.

D: Best to park it somewhere busy, and at night <u>choose a well-lit area</u>.

A: Makes sense. Anything else?

D: Never leave <u>the keys</u> in the car, not even for a second. Don't leave any cash, credit cards, cheque books, mobile phones, vehicle documents or anything, really, <u>where it can be seen</u>.

A: My dad had a hat stolen from the back of his car.

D: A hat?

A: Yeah. Baseball cap.

ANSWER KEY

5 40% (i.e. 100 minus 60)   8 well-lit

6 older (cars)   9 (the) keys

7 car parks   10 can be seen

4.10 LISTENING SCRIPT

(D = Dave; A = Al)

A: So, what did you find out, Dave?

D: Well, if your car gets stolen, you'd think the police would find it eventually, wouldn't you?

A: I suppose so ...

D: Well, according to my research, <u>only 60% of cars are returned to their owners</u>.

A: 60%? What happens to the rest?

D: Who knows? And, listen, I thought it was safer to buy a second-hand car rather than a new one, right?

A: Yeah ...

D: Well, listen to this: '<u>Older cars have a higher probability of being stolen than new ones</u>'. Can you believe it?

A: So, any advice on preventing car crime?

D: Well, don't think that by parking in a car park your car is safe. <u>30% of all car crime happens in car parks</u>.

WRITING

1 Introduction

Aims: To generate interest in the topic of crime and to elicit different opinions about controversial statements.

To introduce students to the idea of justifying why they take a particular point of view.

A ▸ Remind students that the topic of the unit is 'Crime and Punishment'. Read out the statements and ask the class to take a vote (with a show of hands) to see if they agree or disagree.

▸ Have students work individually and indicate their opinion on the scale 1–7.

Support
▸ If students understand the vocabulary, but still do not understand the statements, encourage them to ask questions to elicit the meaning.

B ▸ Put the students into pairs to compare and discuss their answers.

In the exam
▸ Ask students to read the information silently.
▸ Check unknown vocabulary and ask questions on the information to check understanding.
▸ Explain to students that there are two main approaches they can take to a Writing Task 2 'Do you agree or disagree?' essay. They can either write a 'for and against' essay, in which they look at both sides of the argument before presenting a conclusion giving their own opinion, or they can write an 'agree or disagree' essay, in which they write their own opinion from start to finish. 'Agree or disagree' essays are covered in Unit 8.

2 Seeing two sides of an argument

Aims: To introduce the skill of identifying arguments in favour of and against a question or statement.

To provide practice in coming up with arguments for or against a point of view.

A ▸ Have students read through the six opinions on the topic of the death penalty and ask them to identify which opinions are against the death penalty and which are for it. The first one has been done as an example.

▸ Have students work in pairs or individually, and then compare answers.
▸ Check answers as a class.

ANSWER KEY
For: 3, 4, 5   **Against:** 1, 2, 6

Express tip
Read out the advice in this box while students follow in their books. Throughout the rest of this unit, encourage students to use this technique.

B ▸ Put the students into pairs and have them generate and write down arguments for and against the other three opinions listed in the introduction. If there are time limitations, ask students to discuss only one or two of the opinions.

Challenge
▸ Have students read out their arguments for and against the topics in the introduction. The class has to guess if the arguments are for or against and which of the four topics is being commented on.

3 Approaching the question

Aims: To introduce an IELTS Writing Task 2 question and outline a procedure for approaching it, by generating ideas through discussion of the meaning of keywords.

To introduce a technique students can use to generate their own ideas, by providing practice in identifying particular arguments which relate to the different parts of the question.

To get students to appreciate that writing a 'for and against' essay is like two people having an argument. Students learn to make counter-arguments by disagreeing with the points put forward.

A ▸ First, have students read the exam question, then check that they understand the words in the question (especially keywords).

▸ Have students explore the different angles of the question by discussing the subsidiary questions in the speech bubbles in pairs. Encourage students to come up with as many ideas as possible. Explain that brainstorming techniques such as this, are widely used in the workplace, as well as academia, to kick-start the creative process. Tell students that at this stage, we are interested in quantity not quality – all ideas are accepted. Later on, less useful ideas can be rejected.

Express tip

Read out the advice in this box while students follow in their books. Explain that focusing on keywords like this will ensure that students understand exactly what the question is asking, and also help them generate ideas for their essay.

B ▸ Have students read through the opinions in the four speech bubbles, which are all in favour of the question 'Prison is a cure for crime.' Explain that the opinions are all expressed by the woman in the photo – Ms For.

▸ The opinions are all connected to particular keywords in the question – have students match the arguments with these keywords (a–d).

▸ Check answers as a class.

ANSWER KEY
1 b; **2** d; **3** a; **4** c

C ▸ Direct students' attention to the photo of the man and ask them if they think he agrees with what the woman is saying.

▸ Have students take on the role of Mr Against and come up with counter-arguments to respond to each of the four opinions expressed in the speech bubbles. Make sure that, as far as possible, students come up with arguments which are specifically related to the keywords a–d.

Support

▸ If students are finding this activity difficult, refer them back to some of the ideas that were generated in discussing the subsidiary questions in 3A.

Challenge

▸ After students have generated their counter-arguments, ask them to write them down as four separate sentences.

ANSWER KEY
Possible answers include:
1 I totally disagree. The role of prisons is to keep criminals off the streets so it is impossible for them to re-offend!
2 But would you want criminals doing community work helping old people in your family?
3 Prison should be a place of punishment, not some kind of university behind bars.
4 That argument is really not right – if prisoners come out of prison early, they commit more crimes, which is very costly for society.

4 Organising your essay

Aims: To introduce a simple four-part organisational structure for a 'for and against' essay and provide an achievable model essay for intermediate-level students, incorporating the ideas taught in previous exercises.

To teach different language structures for expressing essential functions of 'for and against' essays.

To get students to build arguments, and support and justify opinions and statements about crime, using the language presented in the previous exercise.

A ▸ Explain to students that this essay is a 'good' model essay. There are no grammar mistakes and it fully answers the question. It is not, however, of native speaker standard, as it lacks sufficient cohesion and vocabulary range – many sentences are quite short, there is minimal use of reference words like 'such' and 'these' and vocabulary items such as 'crime' and 'long time' are over-repeated.

▸ Have students read the essay and do the exercise as stated.

ANSWER KEY
1 C; 2 D; 3 A; 4 B

B ▸ Explain to students that this section will deal with language functions – how to contrast an argument, how to introduce a conclusion, etc.

▸ Direct students' attention to the model answer and explain that 'an opposing view' is an example of 'contrasting an argument'.

▸ It's probably best to deal with the answers in chronological order, starting with 'a' and finishing with 's'. To help the students, take them through the first answer as a class – read out the first sentence of the essay and ask them what the function is. If students get the answer wrong, explain why it is wrong and ask them to guess again.

▸ Students will need to re-read the essay to answer the questions and should work individually or in pairs.

▸ Go through the essay point-by-point, highlighting again how it fully answers the question and how ideas are organised and language presented. Encourage students to believe that, whilst it might be unrealistic for them to write an essay without grammar mistakes, replicating this essay type in its other respects is an achievable goal for them.

ANSWER KEY
1 b, f, i, r
2 p
3 e, g, o
4 l, m
5 h, k
6 a, c, d, j, n, s
7 q

C ▸ This section asks students to use the language functions they have just identified to complete the sentences – in sentence 1, students are exposed to 'however' as a function to 'contrast an argument'.

▸ Have students work in pairs or individually to complete the sentences – they will need to come up with their own ideas to answer the questions.

Support
▸ If students find this exercise too difficult, then write the suggested answers in the answer key on the board (mixed up) and have students match them to the correct sentence.

ANSWER KEY
Possible answers are:
1 … the statistics show that crime is still increasing.
2 … there are so many TV programmes and newspaper stories about crime.
3 … community work, where criminals can do something positive for the local community, such as cleaning the streets.
4 … they don't spend enough time on the streets catching criminals.

5 Academic and General Training: Essay

Aims: To give students the opportunity to consolidate the skills introduced in this unit.

To practise a complete Task 2 writing task.

To practise writing within a specified time limit.

For this task
▸ Have students read silently through the summary of points they need to keep in mind when Writing a 'for and against' essay.

▸ After reading, ask students to close their books and tell you in their own words what the points are.

Exam practice
▸ Either set the exam question for homework or do it in class. Depending on the level of the class, you could extend the time limit from 40 to 60 minutes, as this is the first time students will have seen and done a Task 2 Writing task.

▸ When giving feedback to students on their essays, you can also hand out photocopies of the model essay on page 46. Explain to students that the model essay is not a definitive answer – it is one way of answering the question. Stress to students, however, that, like the model in the Coursebook, it is not an authentic native-speaker essay, it is a model essay from a good student – and as such, should be a realistic model that the students themselves can aim for.

Extension: *Identifying language structures*

Aim: *To give further practice at identifying the language structures covered in this unit using the model essay from the teacher's guide.*

Preparation

▶ Make one copy of the model essay for this question from page 46 for every student or pair of students. Alternatively, you can photocopy the essay onto an overhead transparency and do this exercise as a class. This activity will also require students to have copies of their completed writing task for exercise 5.

Procedure

▶ Put the students into pairs or have them work alone.

▶ Have students go through the model essay and identify and underline any language structures that were covered in this unit. Check answers as a class.

▶ Have each student go through their own essay and identify which language structures they have included in their essay, and also any instances where they missed any out.

▶ Get feedback from the class, eliciting examples from individuals of ways in which they could have improved their essays.

Model answer

In discussing how to reduce crime, there are two main approaches of how to deal with this problem – prevention or cure. We can either spend money on more police and prisons in order to control crime, or we can look carefully at why people commit crimes and then attack the causes of crime.

The argument in favour of reducing crime by attacking the causes of crime is that prevention is better than cure. Crime is like a disease, people can either have a vaccination which means they won't develop the disease, or they can take some medicine or antibiotics after they have the disease which will hopefully cure it. Surely it's best not to get the disease in the first place! Following this argument, we need to understand why people commit crimes so the government can develop a strategy to help solve the problems before they become too great.

On the other side of the argument, many people believe that crime can only be reduced by fear and control. If potential criminals know that the police force is excellent, they won't commit crimes because they know they will probably go to prison. Similarly, if they know that all criminals are severely punished with long prison sentences, they will think twice before committing a crime.

In conclusion, I think we need to be hard on criminals, but also hard on the causes of crime. Some people who are very rich and have been given a lot of opportunities in life still commit crime (not paying taxes, for example), so I don't think we can successfully reduce crime only by focussing on the causes of crime.

Transport and Inventions

Section aims:
▸ To help students recognise different types of text maps – ways in which a text is structured.
▸ To provide students with a way of navigating around a text by building a map as they read.
▸ To practise two task types – matching headings to paragraphs and multiple-choice questions.

1 Introduction

Aims: To introduce the topic of flight and to act as a lead-in to the passage.

To elicit some of the transport-related vocabulary which arises later in the unit.

▸ Ask students to discuss the questions in pairs, before they have an open class discussion. In the feedback, make a list of ways of flying on the board, as a way into the text which follows. The list could include the following: *helicopter, glider, hang glider, balloon, kite,* etc.

In the exam

Draw students' attention to the *In the exam* box, which points out the differences between Academic and General Training reading text types. Point out that you are more likely to encounter a text organised as a logical argument in the Academic module than in the General Training module, where the text types are more descriptive or instructive. However, stress that the task types are the same for both modules. The non-argumentative texts may be of a number of patterns. This section will focus on recognising and using these patterns to find your way around a text.

2 Building a mental map of the text

Aims: To introduce the idea of predicting how a text will be structured by reading a number of introductory paragraphs.

To show the different ways in which a text can be structured.

A ▸ When students encounter a text, they have problems identifying the main ideas in each paragraph. In addition to this, they don't see the connections between the ideas and how the ideas relate to the whole text. They therefore find it difficult to locate information which is necessary to answer the questions. They need to see the organisation of the text to understand how it all fits together. Explain to students how building a map will help them to find their way around a text (understand the organisation of the text) and how reading the first paragraph can often offer clues as to how the text will continue in terms of its pattern or structure.

▸ Explain the meaning of the different text types, i.e. categories, chronological description, describing process, building an argument. Have students read the four introductory paragraphs and match them with the types of text map in the table accordingly. Point out to students that it is not necessary to understand all the vocabulary in the paragraphs – they only need to identify the text type.

ANSWER KEY
i 4; ii 1; iii 2; iv 3

B ▸ Have students skim the text to put the inventions in historical order.

ANSWER KEY
1 wings (for birdmen); 2 kites; 3 ornithopter; 4 hot air balloon; 5 glider; 6 propeller planes; 7 jet plane

---

Extension: *Identifying the text type*

Aim: *To provide further practice in identifying the text type, using short articles.*

Preparation
▸ Choose a number of short articles, for which students will identify the text type. Texts can be found on the Internet using search terms such as 'A brief history of ...', 'Different types of ...', 'How to ...'.
▸ Make one copy of each article for each pair of students.

Procedure

‣ Put the students into pairs and give them the articles.

‣ Ask students to decide which of the text types in the Coursebook each article belongs to. Point out that it is possible that a text might fit more than one model.

‣ After each pair has read and analysed their article, have them give feedback to the rest of the group. Feedback should be twofold. Firstly, they should report what the organisational pattern of the text was and secondly, what information they learned from the text.

‣ Place the texts around the room and have students circulate in pairs and skim some or all of the texts to check some of the organisational patterns and main ideas.

3 Rebuilding the text

Aims: To make students aware of the overall structure of a passage by focusing on the main idea in each paragraph and how the ideas fit together.

To give practice in determining suitable headings for paragraphs.

A ‣ Explain how it is important to be clear about the main idea in each paragraph and also to see how the ideas fit together. Have students look at the first two paragraphs only on page 42.

‣ Ask students to choose the main idea for each paragraph from the multiple-choice options. The incorrect choices look at only certain aspects of the paragraph content.

ANSWER KEY

Paragraph A: 3 Flying has a long history

Paragraph B: 2 an ancient Greek legend tells of men flying using birds' wings.

B ‣ After this initial guided practice, have students work out what they think the main idea is in each of the remaining paragraphs. Have them come up with headings and write them on paper.

Support

‣ Offer students two or three possibilities for what the main idea could be for all the paragraphs. The incorrect answers should focus on one aspect of the paragraph and not the main meaning.

Challenge

‣ Have students think of the main idea and a 'wrong answer', i.e. an answer which focuses on one aspect of the paragraph. Students can then test each other on what they think is the main idea.

C ‣ After the students have checked their answers to B with a partner and you have given feedback, ask them to recreate the text by recalling it paragraph-by-paragraph.

4 Matching headings to paragraphs

Aims: To introduce matching headings to paragraphs as a task type.

To give students the opportunity to consolidate the skills introduced in this unit.

For this task

‣ Go through the task rubric in the *For this task* box, stressing that the skills developed in the previous sections will be helpful when dealing with this task.

Exam practice

‣ Ask students to look carefully at the list of headings and focus on the keywords. In the exam, students would skim the text, but this is probably not necessary at this point after the work they have done up to now. Instead, students can use their map of the text to quickly locate the correct paragraphs.

‣ Ask students to cross off the paragraph headings as they select them as answers.

ANSWER KEY

1 x; 2 vi; 3 viii; 4 vii; 5 ix; 6 iv; 7 i; 8 ii

Express tip

Read out the advice in this box while students follow in their books. As with many IELTS tasks, the answer is based on paraphrased information. Use the example in the *Express tip* box to point this out.

Extension: *Writing headings*

Aim: *To provide further practice in identifying suitable headings for paragraphs, through heading writing.*

Preparation

▸ Choose a short article consisting of at least three or four paragraphs. You could re-use one of the articles you brought in for the extension activity 'Identifying the text type'. Make one copy of the article for each pair of students.

Procedure

▸ Put the students into pairs. Give one copy of the article to each pair.

▸ Have students write their own headings for each paragraph, then compare their headings with those of another pair.

▸ Discuss the different headings each pair created with the class, and as a class, decide on the best headings for each paragraph.

5 Multiple-choice questions

Aims: To introduce multiple-choice questions as a task type.

To provide an opportunity for students to use their mental maps of the text to find the information needed to answer the question quickly and efficiently.

A ▸ Point out to your class the usefulness of their map in finding the answer quickly.

▸ Use the example to get students to use the keywords within the question to help them find the correct paragraph. Here, the words 'Greek legend' and 'Icarus' clearly lead students to paragraph B.

ANSWER KEY
9 B

B ▸ Have students focus on similar keywords in questions 10–14 and identify the paragraph which contains the answer before they actually find the answer.

ANSWER KEY
10 C; 11 D; 12 G; 13–14 F

C *For this task*

▸ Before students answer questions 10–14, go through the information in the *For this task* box. Use this opportunity to remind students to draw on their mental maps of the text when looking for the answers, and to explain the stages the students should go through when selecting the correct option.

Exam practice

▸ Have students answer questions 10–14.

ANSWER KEY

10 Answer: D
Note ' ... the first kites were created by the Chinese ...'
11 Answer: A
Note '... the design for da Vinci's machine included many concepts that were later incorporated into the modern-day helicopter.'
12 Answer: D
Note '... Orville piloted the word's first airplane ... '
13, 14 Answer: C / E (in any order)
Note 'Cayley understood two important principles ... airflow over the wings was crucial for producing flight ... any long flight would need an additional, essential ingredient – power.'

5

Section aims:
▸ To introduce some of the types of questions which are asked in Part 3, and teach appropriate language to respond to them beyond 'I think ... ' and 'In my opinion ... '.
▸ To teach students how to give full responses to questions by supporting their opinions.
▸ To practise Part 3 of the Speaking exam – the two-way discussion.

1 Introduction

Aims: To introduce topic-related vocabulary which arises later in the unit.

To encourage students to think deeply about the topic, by making links between transport problems and solutions.

To generate discussion through comparing answers which represent different opinions.

A ▸ Direct students' attention to the photo and ask them if they can identify the train – a Japanese Shinkansen, or Bullet Train. Find out what students know about this train or other high-speed trains in their own countries. Ask them if they think it is better for governments to invest in trains instead of building motorways.

▸ Direct students' attention to the vocabulary in the box and check that they understand any unknown words before doing the exercise.

B ▸ Read through the list of solutions as a class to make sure everyone understands them.

▸ Have students work alone to rank the solutions. Then put the students into small groups where they can share their ranking with the group.

▸ Discuss the rankings as a class.

C ▸ Have students discuss any possible solutions in their groups before sharing their suggestions with the class.

Challenge

▸ Depending on the level of interest in the class, this task can develop into a general discussion on the question of transport in the students' own countries. *What are the main causes of transport problems? Why aren't they being solved? Who is responsible?* etc.

In the exam

Draw students' attention to the *In the exam* box, which provides essential exam information on Speaking Part 3 through a comparison to Part 2.
Have students read through the information silently.

Check any unknown vocabulary. Ask questions to check understanding of content. E.g. *What is the difference between Part 2 and Part 3 of the exam? How long is Part 3?*

2 Identifying types of questions

Aim: To present four common question types which students may be asked in Part 3 of the Speaking exam.

A ▸ Have students match the items in the left and right columns to make grammatically correct questions. Note: Students aren't required to answer the questions at this stage – they will do this later in section 3B.

> **ANSWER KEY**
> 1 d; 2 c; 3 b; 4 a

B ▸ Explain that each of the four questions represents a particular type of Part 3 question. Focus attention on the example answer (compare and contrast) and discuss with students why the question is about discussing differences and similarities.

▸ Ask the students to complete the rest of the exercise by matching each of the remaining three questions to the four question types.

> **ANSWER KEY**
> i 3; ii 1; iii 2; iv 4

3 Giving an appropriate response

Aims: To teach students an extended range of language structures to use when responding to particular examiner question types, and to provide an opportunity to practise them.

To raise awareness of the importance of intonation to show interest and enthusiasm.

A ▸ Before doing the exercise, explain that one of the assessment criteria for the IELTS Speaking exam is 'lexical resource', which grades students according to the appropriacy and range of vocabulary in relation to the task. It is therefore important to go beyond 'I think' and 'In my opinion' to obtain a higher grade.

Support

‣ After completing the exercise, teach (or remind) students of the second conditional to talk about hypothetical situations, by putting some more examples of questions on the board:

How would methods of transport change if the price of oil rose by 400% over the next 5 years?

How would you feel if all new cars sold were fitted with new 'spy technology' which recorded your speed, alcohol consumption, etc?

‣ If students are having real problems with this, refer them to the relevant section of an appropriate grammar book and consider taking time out in the lesson to deal with this.

ANSWER KEY
1 ii; 2 iv; 3 iii; 4 i

B ‣ Have students work in pairs. Ask them to look back at questions 1–4 in 2A. Have each student take turns asking and answering the questions with their partner. Encourage them to use the language from the table in 3A in their answers.

Express tip

Read out the advice in this box while students follow in their books. Explain the function and usefulness of word fillers. Ask students for any equivalent fillers in their language. Have students listen out for these in the recordings of candidate responses and encourage their use in students' own responses.

C ‣ Check students understand what they need to do and then play the recording. Play the recording twice for lower-level groups.

ANSWER KEY
1 Carlos; 2 Raj; 3 Li Lin

5.1 LISTENING SCRIPT

1
(E = Examiner; C = Carlos)

E: What do you think would happen if cities stopped investing in public transport?

C: It would be a big problem.

E: For example?

C: I think workers would spend a lot of time travelling to work.

E: Would there be any other problems?

C: Yes, it wouldn't be good for business – companies want to invest in cities with good public transport.

E: How do you think transport will change in the next 100 years?

C: I think it will change a lot.

E: How?

C: Well, it will depend on a lot of things.

E: What might it depend on?

C: I think it depends a lot on what kind of technological developments happen over the next 100 years.

2
(E = Examiner; R = Raj)

E: What do you think would happen if cities stopped investing in public transport?

R: Well ... I'd imagine there would be a lot of problems. People would waste a lot of time travelling to and from work, which means that the city would not be a very enjoyable place to live in – people's quality of life would certainly get worse.

E: How do you think transport will change in the next 100 years?

R: Well .... It's difficult to say, but maybe with new technology people will work more and more from home, so they won't need to travel so much. In this kind of situation, perhaps transport won't need to change very much at all.

3
(E = Examiner; LL = Li Lin)

E: What do you think would happen if cities stopped investing in public transport?

LL: Mmm ... Well, I think people wouldn't be very happy! There would be more people in cars, more traffic jams and more pollution. Also, cities with poor public transport aren't very good places to do business in, so I think companies wouldn't go there.

E: How do you think transport will change in the next 100 years?

LL: Well ... I think people won't travel very much in the future because they'll be able to experience everything in virtual reality through computers. I think it might be like this computer game I was playing last week ...

Extension: *Using intonation*

Aim: *To provide practice in using intonation and stress patterns to express interest and enthusiasm.*

Preparation

‣ You will need to play recording 5.1. Students will need to be able to read the listening script for this section of the recording, on page 121 of the Coursebook.

Procedure

‣ Play recording 5.1 again to the class, pausing frequently to point out 'good' and 'bad' examples of candidate 2's performance. Chorally repeat 'good' examples. Point out examples of short answers, particularly in Carlos's answers, and elicit from the class ways in which the answer could have been improved.

‣ Put the students into pairs, and have them read the listening script together, paying particular attention to intonation and sounding enthusiastic. They should also be encouraged to extend the conversation and expand upon any short answers.

‣ Monitor and give feedback.

4 Introducing and supporting an opinion

Aims: To provide achievable model examples of candidate performance on the recording so students can start to build a full and comprehensive response to questions.

To encourage students to support their opinions by providing additional information.

A ‣ Give students 30 seconds to study the table of answers.

‣ Play recording 5.2 while students listen and answer the question.

ANSWER KEY

1 No cars in city centre

2 Spend money on roads

3 Speed limit is too low

4 Drivers shouldn't pay higher taxes

5.2 **LISTENING SCRIPT** ——————————

(E = Examiner; C = Candidate)

1

E: What would you think if the government decided to stop people driving in city centres?

C: Mmm, well ... <u>I think it'd be a good idea</u> because there is <u>too much pollution</u> produced by cars and also there is too much traffic on the roads. In my home city there is a very good public transport system, for example, so people can always take the bus or subway.

2

E: Do you think the government should spend more money on building roads or railways?

C: Well ... people prefer taking their cars than taking the train, <u>so for me, building roads is more important</u>. In my country, for example, <u>the trains are often so crowded that nobody really wants to go by train.</u>

3

E: Do you think we should increase the maximum speed limit for cars?

C: <u>Yes! I completely agree</u> – the speed limit is too low in towns and cities – especially at night when there is so little traffic and no children on the streets. Also, the motorway speed limit in Japan is crazy – I really think <u>we should do the same as Germany</u> and have no speed limits on motorways. It works fine there.

4

E: Some people say that car drivers should pay higher taxes if they have bigger cars. What would you say?

C: Yeah ... <u>I tend to disagree</u>. In my view, people should pay more tax because they earn more money, not because they have a bigger car. <u>Somebody could have a big *old* car which is very *cheap* – why should they pay more than someone with a small *new* car which is very *expensive*?</u>

B ‣ Play recording 5.2 a second time for students to complete the second and third column of the table.

‣ Check answers for the whole table by playing the recording a third time, pausing after each answer to check it. Point out to students that they may need to check more than one box for each item.

ANSWER KEY

1 I think it'd be a good idea; Too much pollution

2 For me, ... is more important; People prefer cars; Example of uncomfortable trains in home country

---

3 I completely agree; Example of another country

4 I tend to disagree; Logical explanation why higher taxes are unfair

C ▸ Encourage students to think of their local area and use their own experience and knowledge to answer the questions and not simply repeat the answers they have heard on the recording. Do they agree or disagree with the candidates answers? Why/Why not?

5 Two-way discussion

Aims: To provide a summary of learning points encountered in the section which will need to be employed to answer the following exam practice questions.

To provide an opportunity for students to practise Part 3 of the Speaking exam, and to consolidate the skills introduced in this unit.

For this task

Ask students to read the information silently and memorise it. Ask them to close their books and tell you in their own words what the key points are. Write them up on the board in note form for reinforcement.

Exam practice

▸ Check that students understand the vocabulary in the box and pre-teach as necessary before doing the task in pairs. Encourage students to write a variety of questions using different question types. Students do NOT answer the questions at this stage.

▸ Check that all students have at least 4 questions written down before asking and answering the questions in pairs. If students have trouble thinking of questions, provide examples, either individually or as a class on the board, to ensure they have a full complement of questions.

▸ For further work on Speaking Part 3 of the exam, refer to the *IELTS Express Video/DVD* which accompanies the book.

ANSWER KEY

Possible answers include:

1 What do you think are the main causes of car accidents? (speculate)

2 Do you think people should have to wear seatbelts only in the front of the car or in the back of the car, too? (comparative)

3 Many people believe that regular driving tests is the best way to improve road safety – do you agree? (evaluate)

4 Would drivers in your country obey the law if the government stopped them from using mobile phones? (hypothesise)

Extension: *Dialogue building*

Aim: *To provide additional practice in asking and answering questions of the types in the previous exercise.*

Preparation

▸ During the Exam practice section in Section 5, circulate and take note of the students' questions to each other.

Procedure

▸ Once students have finished the speaking activity in Section 5, write on the board the list of questions that you identified.

▸ Ask students to identify the types of questions noted (hypothesise, speculate, etc).

▸ Choose one or two questions and use them as a starting point to build a dialogue, eliciting questions and answers from the class. Write the questions and answers on the board as you go.

▸ Put the students into pairs, and have them work together to construct similar dialogues using other questions on the board as a starting point. Choose several pairs to read their dialogues to the class.

▸ As you monitor this activity, note down student errors to put up on the board at the end of the activity for error correction work. It is good practice to take note of the students' errors as whole sentences, not simply isolated words.

⬜ IELTS Express Speaking Video

If you are using the *Speaking Video* which accompanies *IELTS Express*, Section 3 – Part 2 of the video relates to the content of this unit. The video could either be shown at the beginning of this lesson to give students a general idea of the content and format of Part 3 of the IELTS Speaking exam, or alternatively, it could be shown at the end of the lesson to provide a recap and demonstration of the material covered in this unit. For more information on the *IELTS Express Speaking Video DVD* and how to integrate it into your lessons, see page 103.

The Natural World

Section aims:
- To give students practice in identifying speakers in conversations with more than two speakers.
- To develop students' skill in identifying the opinions and attitude of a particular speaker.
- To give further practice in Listening Section 3: Academic dialogue.
- To practise a number of task types – classification; table completion and summary completion.

1 Introduction

Aims: To indirectly introduce the topics of the natural world and the environment, and to elicit some of the vocabulary which arises later in the unit.

To introduce the idea of agreeing or disagreeing with controversial statements.

A ▸ Draw students' attention to the photograph and the quotation at the start of the unit.

▸ Ask a student to read out the quotation or do so yourself. Check for any unknown vocabulary and make sure students understand the meaning and implications of the quote. Elicit suggestions for what the speaker means.

▸ Biographical note on J Krishnamurti:
Born in South India in 1895, eighth child of middle class family. Educated privately in England. Later he returned to India. The core of Krishnamurti's teaching is contained in the statement he made in 1929, when he said: *'Truth is a pathless land. Man cannot come to it through any organisation, through any creed, through any dogma, priest or ritual, not through any philosophic knowledge or psychological technique. He has to find it through the mirror of relationship, through the understanding of the contents of his own mind ... '* (http://www.jkrishnamurti.org). Died in 1986.

B ▸ Have students work in pairs to discuss whether they agree or disagree with the quote.

▸ Elicit a few opinions from students in the class. You could build this up to a class discussion.

In the exam
Draw students' attention to the *In the exam* box. Give them a few minutes to read it through for themselves, before reading it aloud, explaining vocabulary and checking understanding where necessary.

2 Identifying attitude

Aims: To give students practice in identifying attitude of speakers.

To increase awareness of a range of expressions signifying agreement, disagreement, interest, confusion and disbelief.

A ▸ Tell students they will hear 4 short statements. The speakers will express the ideas (a–d), but will use different words to those printed in the Coursebook. Ask students to listen to the conversations and number them in the order they hear them.

▸ Play recording 6.1.

ANSWER KEY
1 d; 2 b; 3 c; 4 a

6.1 LISTENING SCRIPT

A: I don't think it's right that animals are kept in captivity.

B: Doing tests on animals is morally wrong, I feel.

C: We are so wasteful! We ought to only eat produce from our own region at the time of year it is naturally available.

D: It's not my job to look after the environment. What do I pay my taxes for?

B ▸ Tell students they should now focus on the response to each statement. Ask them to draw a line between each statement and its response. Warn them that they should pay particular attention to the start of each response.

▸ Play recording 6.2.

Support

▸ If you think your students may find this activity difficult, pause the recording after the first exchange to check answers. Then play the remaining three exchanges.

6.2 LISTENING SCRIPT

1

A: I don't think it's right that animals are kept in captivity.

B: Absolutely. I couldn't agree with you more.

2

A: Doing tests on animals is morally wrong, I feel.

B: Yeah, but a lot of important discoveries have come out of that research, you know ...

3

A: We are so wasteful! We ought to only eat produce from our own region at the time of year it is naturally available.

B: 'Naturally available?' I'm not sure I follow you ...

4

A: It's not my job to look after the environment. What do I pay my taxes for?

B: What!? You can't be serious! Don't you know every little bit helps?

C ▸ Tell students that in each of the conversations, the second speaker responds with a different attitude. For example, in the first conversation, the second speaker agrees with the first. Play the first conversation again, as an example.

▸ Now play the remaining 3 conversations and have students identify the attitude of the second speaker. Have students check their answers in pairs.

▸ When you check the answers, you may wish to ask for the exact wording of the response. Write them up on the board. Point out the possible confusion which may arise in 'Absolutely. I couldn't agree with you more.' Students may think this is negative ('couldn't agree'). Tell them it means 'I agree with you a lot'. Also stress that 'Yeah, but ...' means 'NO!'

▸ Take this opportunity to drill the intonation by playing recording 6.2 again, pausing after each response and asking students to repeat the intonation on the recording.

D ▸ Copy the table from the Coursebook onto the board. Ask students if they can remember any of the responses from recording 6.2. Ask them which column the responses would go in.

▸ Tell students to construct a similar table in their notebooks. Then, working in small groups rather than pairs, they should try to think of different ways of expressing these 5 attitudes.

▸ As they work, circulate, correcting mistakes and feeding in ideas (see below).

▸ After five minutes, elicit feedback from students and record their ideas in the table on the board.

▸ You could take this opportunity to clear up the common student error of 'I am (dis)agree with you'! It's either 'I agree with you' OR 'I am in agreement with you'.

Support

▸ Less confident groups could simply sort a list of expressions into attitudes. You could put the following expressions on the board or on a handout (but don't forget to jumble them up!).

Extension: *Responding with attitude*

Aim: *To provide further practice with expressions showing attitude, by having students practise these responses in an open chain round the class.*

Procedure

▸ Tell the students to write down two or three statements related to the unit topic that not everyone would agree with. For example, *Meat is Murder. We should all stop eating meat; Chimpanzees should be given the same rights as humans;* or *People's welfare should be placed above the welfare of animals,* etc.

▸ Invite one student to read out one of their statements to another student on the other side of the class. The second student then has to respond to the statement showing their own opinion, using one of the expressions introduced earlier in the unit. Continue until each student has had an opportunity to respond to another student's statement and present one of their own.

E ▸ Put students into small groups of 3 or 4. Tell them that they are now to discuss the opinions stated in 2A. Tell them to ask their partners whether they agree or not and why they feel like this. Give them an example, e.g. opinion a: *I agree with this statement. It is not private individuals that cause the most damage to the environment, it is big business. The government has to pass laws to regulate these organisations.*

▸ Circulate and monitor, taking a note of any problem areas or interesting opinions and feed in new vocabulary as needed.

▸ After 5 minutes or so, bring the class back together as a group. Highlight and correct any common errors you heard and invite certain students to tell the group any particularly interesting or coherent opinions you heard earlier. Invite other students to comment and build into a group discussion.

3 Identifying Speakers

Aim: To give students practice in identifying speakers in conversations with three speakers.

A ▸ On the board, write *Zoos*. Then, underneath, create two columns, headed *Advantages* and *Disadvantages*.

Ask students to copy these headings on to a sheet of paper. Check they all know what a zoo is! Ask students to work in groups of three to brainstorm advantages and disadvantages of zoos.

▸ After a few minutes, ask for their ideas and put them up on the board. This list will be referred to later, in the extension activity following 3B.

▸ Tell students that in Section 3 of the exam, they are often presented with a three-way conversation and have to identify 'who says what'. This is particularly difficult because unlike on TV or in real life, you can't see who is talking, and there are usually at least two people of the same gender.

▸ Tell students they should listen particularly carefully at the beginning of the recording, when a speaker will often use the other speakers' names. Tell them not to worry about correctly identifying the accent – it doesn't really matter if they are from Manchester or Manhattan – they just need to know they are different!

▸ Play the first few lines of recording 6.3. Keep stopping the recording at random in the middle of each turn and ask the students *Who is this speaking now?* Check their answers against the listening script.

▸ Ask students to make a note of how many times each person talks, by putting a tick in the relevant box in exercise 3A. Then rewind back to the beginning of the recording and play it all the way through.

▸ Check answers as a class.

ANSWER KEY
Cedric speaks 6 times (Amina speaks 4 times, Dr Bannister 6)

6.3 LISTENING SCRIPT
(DB = Dr. Bannister; C = Cedric; A = Amina;)

DB: Hello. For those who don't know me, my name is Ray Bannister. Anyway, welcome to today's Life Sciences seminar. Now, this term we'll be looking at the relationship between man and animals. Let's start by looking at zoos. Have you ever been to a zoo, Cedric?

C: Yes, lots of times. They used to take us on day trips when we were at school.

DB: And what do you think of zoos? Are they a good thing, do you think?

C: Oh, yes. All the lions and tigers and snakes. It's great fun.

DB: But many people are critical of zoos. Why is that, Amina?

A: Well, I don't like zoos. Zoos turn animals into a sideshow. Animals should be free to live their lives. If you put an animal in a cage, you take away its dignity.

C: Yes, but, Amina, zoos allow people to see and learn about animals.

A: That's true. But we can see animals and learn about them from the television.

C: But that's no substitute for seeing the real thing.

DB: Ok. Let's look at other aspects of zoos' work. Is it not true that many zoos actually help to preserve some endangered species?

C: That's right. At my local zoo, you can help animals by adopting an animal. You get news on how it's doing and pictures and everything. We sponsored an orangutan at my school.

A: But some zoos actually make the situation worse by taking an animal out of the wild. Surely it would be better to leave it where it is?

DB: Well, Amina, that's not necessarily the case. Many animals are hunted and many natural habitats are being destroyed and if the animals were left there, they would die.

C: Yeah, and zoos run breeding programmes to increase the numbers of particular species.

A: OK. I agree. Zoos do some useful work. But what upsets me is seeing those poor animals in those tiny cages. They have no space to run around and they get stressed being kept in a cage all day.

DB: But in recent years many zoos have got rid of the cages and given the animals more space to move around. And then, of course, there are safari parks. Has anyone ever been to a safari park?

B
▸ Tell students they must match the information or opinions to the speakers. Ask them to look at questions 1–4 and identify the keywords.
▸ Play recording 6.3 without stopping. Have students record their answers as they listen. Remind them they only have to write A, B or C, not the full names.
▸ Afterwards, let students check their answers against the listening script in the back of their books.

ANSWER KEY
1 C; 2 C; 3 B; 4 A

Express tip

Read out the advice in this box while students follow in their books. Explain to students that when there are three people speaking, they may have similar voices. Using the technique outlined in the tip will help them keep track of who is speaking at any time.

Extension: *Agreeing and disagreeing*

Aim: To give students practice in using the language of agreement and disagreement.

Preparation
▸ You will need to use the list of advantages and disadvantages of zoos that was made on the board earlier. If you didn't do this stage, it should be done now.
▸ Students will need to have heard recording 6.3 and to have before them the listening script on pages 122–123 of the Coursebook.

Procedure
▸ Ask students which of the advantages and disadvantages of zoos they listed on the board earlier were mentioned in the conversation. Can they add any more advantages or disadvantages to their list?
▸ Choose 3 students to model the conversation in recording 6.3 for the class, so you can correct pronunciation and intonation, then put the students into groups of 3 and have them perform the conversation together.
▸ Now ask them to extend the conversation to include any of the advantages and disadvantages that are not already included in recording 6.3. They can either write out this extension and then act it out or improvise it. Circulate and feed in new language.
▸ Ask some groups to read out their extensions to the rest of the class.

4 Classification

Aims: To introduce classification as a task type.

To give further practice in Section 3 of the exam.

For this task
▸ Ask students to read through the box, highlighting the main ideas.

▸ Write the word *vivisection* on the board. Ask what it means. Give a dictionary definition, e.g. *an operation performed on an animal for medical research*. Check the understanding of the word by asking concept checking questions, such as:

Is everyone in favour of vivisection? (no)

Are lions and giraffes often used for vivisection? (no)

What kinds of animals are used? (rats, rabbits, monkeys, cats, etc.)

Who usually performs vivisection? (scientists, medical researchers, etc.)

Where is it done?

Express tip

Read out the advice in this box while students follow in their books. Explain that because the information on the recording comes in the same order as the questions, they will know if they have missed the answer to a particular question. If this is the case, they should keep going on to the next question so they don't miss that one, too.

Exam practice

▸ Have students read through Questions 1–7 and highlight or underline the keywords. Check what they think the keywords are (*ill, survey, supports, rights, advances, cosmetics, computer simulation*).

▸ Ask if they can think of any synonyms for these keywords.

▸ Check they understand what is required of them.

▸ Play recording 6.4.

▸ Check answers.

Support

▸ Pre-teach some vocabulary. Language you may wish to pre-teach includes: *to do tests/experiments, to have rights, to be treated well, to be abused, to force someone to do something, Alzheimer's disease, medical technology, computer-simulated models, cell research*.

▸ You could give additional support by stopping the recording in the middle of each line and asking who is talking. Also stop the recording after each keyword, ask students to record their answers and move on to the next keyword.

ANSWER KEY
1 B; 2 B; 3 A; 4 C; 5 A; 6 C; 7 C

6.4 LISTENING SCRIPT

(E = Eddie; D = Dawn; F = Fran;)

E: Hi, Dawn.

D: Oh, hi, Eddie. How are you?

E: OK now. Last month I was ill for several days but I'm much better now.

D: What was the matter?

E: Well, the doctors weren't sure. They did several tests but couldn't find anything wrong with me. But I'm fine now. Look, can you spare a few minutes? I'm doing a survey on people's attitudes towards vivisection. It's for my assignment.

D: Yeah. OK. Oh ... this is Fran, she's in my study group.

E: Hi, Fran. I'm Eddie. Pleased to meet you.

F: Hello, Eddie.

D: What's it about again?

E: Vivisection. You know, doing experiments on live animals. Are you for or against vivisection?

D: Well, for, I suppose.

E: OK. That's one for ...

F: You don't mean you support vivisection, Dawn? It's horrible what they do to those poor animals.

D: But new drugs and treatments have to be tested, Fran. I mean, you couldn't ask a person to take a lot of untested drugs. They might die.

F: But that's just it. A person could refuse. People have the right to choose what they want to do, and so should animals.

E: So, you think animals should have rights?

F: Yes. Animals have just as much right to life as we have, and they have the right to be treated well, you know, and not abused in this way.

E: You obviously feel quite strongly on this. What about you, Dawn?

D: In a perfect world, I'd agree with you, Fran. But it's not a perfect world. For example, take your mystery illness, Eddie. Perhaps animal research could help with that.

F: Yeah, but he's better now.

D: That's not the point. What if he was an old man or a small child? Some people might not get better as easily as he did.

F: What's that got to do with keeping animals in tiny cages in a lab and performing lots of horrible experiments on them? Do you know they force dogs to smoke? It's horrible.

D: It may be horrible Fran, but the fact is that the research could save lives. You know, great advances in Alzheimer's disease have been made through animal research.

E: OK, but do you think all animal research is valid, Dawn?

D: What do you mean?

E: Well, just because something works with a rat or a monkey doesn't necessarily mean it works on humans. We're different physically. So do you support all animal experiments?

D: Well, I ...

F: And as for testing cosmetics on animals! Do you know they deliberately put shampoo into rabbits' eyes just to see what happens? I mean, who needs a new shampoo? The ones in the shops work just fine.

D: Um, yeah, I take your point ...

F: What's more, we don't need to use animals these days. Medical technology is so advanced, they can use computer simulated models or cell research. They don't need a whole animal.

D: Well ... That's true ...

E: OK. Thank you both very much. You've given me some really interesting ideas. Bye now!

D: Any time.

F: Bye.

Extension: *Discussion*

Aim: *To give students the opportunity to use the language of agreement and disagreement in the context of a class discussion on vivisection.*

Preparation
▸ Students will need to have heard recording 6.4 and to have before them the listening script on pages 123–124 of the Coursebook.

Procedure
▸ Play recording 6.4 again. Have students follow using the listening script in the back of their books.
▸ Ask students if anyone 'won' this argument. Ask who they agreed with most, Fran or Dawn.
▸ Put the students into two groups; those who are opposed to vivisection and those who aren't. Explain that it doesn't matter what their own opinion really is. Give each group a number of minutes to prepare arguments for their position on the argument.
▸ Encourage a class discussion by selecting individual students to present their position. If necessary, act as 'devil's advocate' by deliberately presenting an argument in order to provoke a response. Encourage students to use the language of agreement and disagreement in the text to respond to the previous speaker's views.

---

5 Table completion; summary completion

Aim: To introduce table completion and summary completion as task types.

For this task
▸ Read through the stages in the *For this task* box with your students.
▸ Tell students they will now do a table completion task.

A Exam practice
Questions 1–12
▸ Ask the students to read the rubric on page 50.
▸ Play recording 6.5 and have students answer the questions.
▸ Afterwards, let students check their answers against the listening script, then with you.

Support
▸ You may wish to pre-teach all or some of the following vocabulary: *lion, lioness, tiger, leopard, cheetah, ocelot, big cats, domestic cats, cubs, king of the jungle, elephant, gazelle, zebra, springbok, wildebeest, warthog, elephant, rodents, reptiles, greyhound, creature, paws, tail, mane, fur, stripes, spots, to hunt, prey, predator, to pounce, endangered, extinct.*

ANSWER KEY

1 250; **2** Africa; **3** two or more; **4** zebra; **5** females;
6 nearly extinct; **7** (work) in groups; **8** 110; **9** 6;
10 Chile; **11** forests; **12** (their) paws

6.5 **LISTENING SCRIPT**

(T = Teacher; D = Donna; K = Kyle)

T: Good afternoon, everyone. This week's presentation is from Donna and Kyle. Ready?

D, K: Yes. Just about ...

T: OK. Away you go. And we'll do a q and a when you finish.

D: Good afternoon. Even as children, most of us can recognise some of the cat family: the tiger with his stripes; the leopard with his spots; the lion with his mane. But how much do we really know about them and their behaviour? Let's look at three quite distinct members of the cat family. First, the only one of our three cats not endangered – the lion, the king of the jungle. Why is he the king? First, his sheer physical presence. An adult male can weigh anything <u>between 160 and 250 kilograms</u>. No wonder they're called big cats! Secondly, there may be heavier or even bigger animals on <u>the plains of Africa</u>, the elephant, for example, but when it comes to hunting and killing, few can match the lion.

K: Actually, the male is not the biggest predator. It's the female, the lioness.

D: That's right. Lionesses often work in small groups, usually <u>two or more</u>, to corner and kill their prey – gazelle, <u>zebra</u>, wildebeest or buffalo.

K: But when the lionesses are off hunting, who looks after the cubs?

D: Ah hah, it's the females again! <u>Rearing the cubs is a shared responsibility for the females</u> of the pride.

K: So, if the lionesses kill most of the food and look after all the cubs, why is the male king of the animals?

D: Good question, Kyle.

K: Yes ... well, moving on from the king of the animals to the fastest – certainly on dry land.

D: The cheetah. A truly beautiful creature. Unfortunately, endangered and <u>nearly extinct</u>.

K: Built for speed, its greyhound-like body is very light for its size, weighing merely 30 to 50 kilograms. Its long tail gives it its distinctive shape and helps it balance better when it's on the move.

D: Cheetahs are found in Africa, the Middle East and South Central Asia. Unlike the lion, cheetahs are usually solitary hunters, though they will <u>occasionally work in groups</u> in order to bring down larger prey such as buffalo. Other prey include springbok, warthog and gazelle.

K: What's most impressive about the cheetah is its speed. It can reach <u>a speed of a hundred and ten kilometres per hour</u> in only a matter of seconds.

D: Finally, the ocelot, one of the smallest of the 'Big Cats'. There, isn't he cute? They weigh <u>as little as 6 kilograms</u> – that's only as much as some domestic cats. Sadly, the ocelot too, is threatened with extinction through habitat loss and being hunted for its beautiful fur. It is found in most South

American countries, <u>with the exception of Chile</u>, and also in Central America and some southern US states.

K: The lion and the cheetah both live and hunt in open plains. The solitary ocelot prefers to live and <u>hunt in forests</u>. Here they catch rodents, reptiles and even fish.

D: Uhm ... They have an interesting technique for fishing, too, <u>using their paws to flip fish out of the water</u> and then pounce on them.

K: So, there you are, three quite distinct but all equally amazing members of the cat family.

T: Fascinating! Any questions?

Extension: *Pyramid discussion*

Aim: To provide an opportunity for discussion, using the context of the reasons for and consequences of extinction in the animal kingdom.

Preparation

▶ Write the following questions on the board:
What other 'Big Cats' are there?
What other animals are in danger of extinction?
Why are their numbers declining?
What is being done to stop this decline?
What else can we do?
Why should or shouldn't we do something?

Procedure

▶ Put students into pairs. Ask each pair to discuss the questions on the board.
▶ After a few minutes, put two pairs together to form a group of four and tell them to discuss the same questions again.
▶ After 10 minutes or so, put the fours together to form eights and discuss the questions again. Keep doing this till the whole class is involved in one big discussion.
▶ Meanwhile, you can circulate, monitor and feed in new language as needed.

B Exam practice
Questions 1–6

▶ Tell students that they will now do a summary completion task. This is almost identical to the notes completion tasks, which they have already encountered in Unit 4. The only difference here is that all the sentences are presented in the context of a paragraph (or two) and that there are some sentences which do not require completion. However, the approach is the same, namely:

a Read the instructions.

b Skim through the text.

c Identify each question and answer-type.

d Identify keywords and paraphrasing.

e Try to predict the answer.

f Listen carefully for the keywords and record the answers while listening.

g Check spelling and the number of words for each answer.

▶ Play recording 6.6 straight through, thus giving the students some exam-style practice.

Express tip

Read out the advice in this box while students follow in their books. Remind students that they are given 10 minutes at the end of the listening exam to transfer their answers to the answer sheet. They should always use this time to check the spelling of all their answers.

ANSWER KEY

1 oxygen; 2 animals and plants; 3 industrial; 4 nests;
5 pollution; 6 chemicals

6.6 LISTENING SCRIPT ────────

(W = Wayne; B = Becky)

W: Hi, Becky.

B: Oh! Hi, Wayne. You weren't at the Environmental Studies lecture this morning ...

W: No, I er ... Did I miss anything?

B: 'Factors influencing river life' and Doctor Bellamy set us an essay.

W: Oh no!

B: Don't worry. I took some notes. Now, listen carefully. A river's speed will dictate which animals and plants can survive in it. Got that? Usually, the faster the water, the more oxygen it contains. That's good for life. But fast-flowing rivers are more difficult to swim in, so some animals prefer more mature, slower rivers.

W: Slower rivers ...

B: Now, on its journey from its source to the sea, a river may pass over several different types of substrate: clay, sandst ...

W: Substrate?

B: The layers of rock beneath it. Clay, sandstone, chalk, soft or hard limestone, etc. Anyway, each kind of rock has an influence on the mineral content of the water and the species of animals and plants that are able to survive there.

W: Er, mineral content?

B: For instance, the freshwater crayfish requires water with plenty of oxygen and a good supply of lime to help create and maintain its thick, outer skeleton. So, a fast-flowing river running over chalk is perfect.

W: Chalk, right ...

B: Another factor is man. In the past, some rivers have been used as transportation channels by large industrial boats. In fact, some still are. So, many stretches of river have had to be deeply dredged – dug out – to maintain a deep channel. This prevents the bottom of the river developing naturally.

W: Right ...

B: What's more, smaller craft need water plants such as lilies, reeds and rushes to be removed ...

W: Otherwise they get all caught up in the propellers!

B: That's right! But their removal means that there is less habitat for wildlife. What's more, fast motor boats create wash that causes the erosion of the river banks, floods the nests of animals and washes away wildlife.

W: That's terrible! All those little water rats and birds!

B: The last main factor, Wayne, is pollution.

W: I never drop any litter; I ...

B: Unfortunately, it's not people like you or me that are mainly responsible for river pollution.

W: No?

B: The commonest kinds of pollution are industrial and include sewage; chemicals and other waste created by industry; fertilisers and pesticides; litter; large amounts of hot water; dense or decaying plant growth and, finally, slurry – that's animal waste.

W: Animal waste. Right. Thanks, Becky. When's this essay got to be in?

B: Friday.

W: Friday! Guess I'd better get to the library.

Section aims:

▸ To introduce and practise language used to describe trends, including verbs, nouns, adverbs, and adjectives.

▸ To provide practice in extracting information from line and bar graphs showing trends.

▸ To provide further practice with Academic Writing Task 1 of the IELTS Writing exam.

1 Introduction

Aims: To introduce the topic of weather and climate trends.

To introduce students to the skill of extracting information from graphs showing trends.

A ▸ Either put students in pairs to answer the first two questions or ask the questions to the class as a whole. Try to elicit a few examples of target language structures as students talk about how weather changes throughout the year, e.g. *There's a big increase in rain in August.*

ANSWER KEY

Left: New Delhi; top right: Singapore; bottom right: Cairo

B ▸ Students can do this exercise individually or in pairs. If they do it individually, ask them to compare their answers in pairs.

ANSWER KEY

1 The table represents average monthly rainfall over the year in three cities. The line graph represents average monthly temperatures over the year in the three cities.

2 Temperature is measured in degrees Celsius; rainfall is measured in millimetres.

3 New Delhi has the highest temperature in a year. Cairo has the lowest.

4 Singapore has the highest rainfall in a year. Cairo has the lowest.

In the exam

Draw students' attention to the *In the exam* box. Ask students to read the information silently. Check unknown vocabulary and ask questions on the information to check understanding. For example:

How long should you spend writing Task 1?

What's the minimum number of words you should write?

2 Using the language of trends

Aims: To introduce a range of nouns and verbs used to describe the direction of trends.

To introduce a range of adverbs and adjectives used to describe the size and degree of trends.

To encourage students to discover the grammar used in the model writing so they will be able to reproduce this in their own writing.

To provide writing practice using the target language taught in relation to a line graph showing monthly temperatures.

A ▸ Give students a few moments to look at the table, then do the first example as an open question to the class.

▸ Have students continue individually or in pairs. If working individually, they should compare their answers in pairs afterwards.

ANSWER KEY

1 rise, increase …; 2 fall, drop …; 3 reach a peak …; 4 fall to a low point …; 5 remain stable …; 6 fluctuate, move up and down …

B ▸ Tell students that this is NOT a grammar exercise – for them to correctly identify the answers they will need to refer to and understand the table showing monthly rainfall.

ANSWER KEY

In Singapore, the amount of rainfall **drops dramatically** from January to February. After a **slight rise** in March, the level of rainfall **decreases steadily** until July. Over the next three months, the rainfall **fluctuates sharply**. Finally, at the end of the year, we can see a **dramatic rise** in rainfall in November and a **peak** in December.

In Cairo, the rainfall **remains constant** at 5mm per month from January to March. It then **declines gradually** to zero in July and August before **rising gradually** again in the second half of the year.

In New Delhi, there is a **steady drop** in rainfall from January to March followed by a **dramatic increase** to around 170–180mm in July and August. The final part of the year shows rainfall **falling dramatically** to a **low point** of 3mm in November.

C ▸ When checking the answers to these questions, ask students to underline some examples in the model paragraphs.

ANSWER KEY
1 F 2 T 3 F

Extension: *Identifying the tense of graphs*

Aim: *To provide further practice in identifying the correct tense required to discuss information in a graph.*

Preparation

▸ You will need to draw some graphs on the board. You might wish to prepare these ahead of time and draw them on a piece of paper which you could copy and hand out. Alternatively, you could bring in a selection of graphs cut from newspapers. The main thing is that the graphs require a variety of tenses to describe them.

Procedure

▸ Present your graphs to the students and ask them what tense they would use in each one. For example, draw a line graph showing annual profits for a newspaper company from 1994 to 2004 ($ on vertical axis, years on horizontal) – past tense. Another example graph might show monthly ice cream sales with no particular reference to a year (sales volume in 000s on vertical axis, months on horizontal) – present simple.

D ▸ Ask students to use the model paragraphs as a guide to help them with their writing. Point out that they need to use a variety of language in their descriptions – not just verb constructions using the same verb.

Express tip

Read out the advice in this box while students follow in their books. Again, remind students of the importance of taking a few minutes before they begin to write, to identify what the most important or interesting features of the graph are.

3 Describing trends

Aims: To provide an opportunity for students to use the language of trends by completing a gap-fill activity which describes a bar chart.

To get students to discover lexical and structural features of the model paragraph which they can later use in their own writing.

To encourage students to correctly use the prepositions commonly used in relation to graphs and in particular, trends.

To provide writing practice for students, using the language presented with reference to a block line graph.

A ▸ Give students 30 seconds to look at the graphs and understand them. Ask the following comprehension questions before getting students to do the task. *What do the graphs show?* (average monthly temperature and rainfall in two cities – Entebbe and Alice Springs) *What does the bar chart/block line graph show?* (The bars show rainfall, the block line graph shows temperature.)

ANSWER KEY
1 very little; 2 gradually; 3 rising; 4 fluctuates; 5 sharp; 6 reaching a peak; 7 a low point; 8 no change; 9 increase

B ▸ When checking the answers, impress on students that it is not always necessary to be overly specific with numbers in a report. Rounding numbers up or down and using words such as 'approximately' makes the description easier to follow for the reader and is therefore far more communicative.

ANSWER KEY
1 On the other hand; 2 about, approximately

C ▸ Have students complete the sentences with the correct preposition from the box.

ANSWER KEY
1 from, to, over; 2 From, to, in; 3 Between, of; 4 by; 5 in; in

Express tip

Read out the advice in this box while students follow in their books. Remind students that they should, of course, only use these expressions when talking about graphs that show data up to the present day.

Extension: *Using the correct tense*

Aim: *To reinforce the use of different tenses used to discuss different graphs.*

Preparation

▸ This activity uses the 5 sentences in Section 3C – the 'Global Warming' box. Students should have already completed this exercise.

Procedure

▸ After completing 3C, draw students' attention to the fact that each sentence is written with a different tense. Ask them to identify the tense and tell you why that tense is being used.

ANSWER KEY

1 Future with *will* for predictions

2 Past simple for time – referenced period in the past

3 Present perfect – the writer wrote this sentence in 2004 – i.e. a period of time starting in the past and continuing to the present

4 Present continuous to talk about developing and changing situations

5 Present simple to describe facts

D ▸ Before students start writing, quickly remind them of the language and model format they have been using to describe rainfall, and let them know you will be expecting to see them use it in their own descriptions of temperature graphs. An example model paragraph might be:

Turning to temperature, the graphs show that in Entebbe, the temperature remains relatively constant throughout the year. In January, the temperature stands at approximately 38 degrees and falls gradually to a low point of about 36 degrees in August, before rising again slowly in the second part of the year. Alice Springs, on the other hand, has a much more variable climate in terms of temperature. Similar to Entebbe, the temperature in January is around 35 degrees, but this falls much more sharply to a low point of about 28

degrees in June. Like Entebbe, the second half of the year shows a rise in temperature to reach the same level as at the beginning of the year.

4 Academic Writing Task 1: Report

Aims: To give students the opportunity to consolidate the skills introduced in this unit.

To practise a complete Task 1 Writing task.

To practise writing within a specified time limit.

For this task

▸ Like all *For this task* boxes, this is a summary of the skills the students have practised in this section and which they should apply when completing the *Exam practice* section that follows.

▸ Have students read through the *For this task* box. Ask them if anything is unclear or they have any questions. Refer them back to the relevant skills section in the unit to connect the summary point in the *For this task* box.

▸ Emphasise to students that you expect them to apply these points to their essay writing!

▸ As with all writing and reading exam practice questions, you can either set this for homework or do it as a timed piece of work in class.

Support

▸ If the general language level is low and/or students are still having problems interpreting graphs, it might be a good idea to discuss the graph as a class before students write the report.

▸ Start by discussing what CFCs are and how they affect the environment – use the information in the footnote to help here. Then ask comprehension questions about the chart *What's the graph about? What do the axes represent?* etc. In particular, ask them to identify the key information before they start rushing into descriptions: In general, *Is the picture a positive or negative one for the world's environment? Which country is the odd one out?* (Ukraine) are the key questions here. If you need to help students further, then give them an extra 10 minutes to complete the task – 30 minutes instead of the 20 minutes suggested.

Model answer

The line graph shows the amount of CFC emissions from four different countries in the world from 1989 to 2002.

The main point to note from the graph is that CFC emissions have gone down in all countries except the Ukraine. Although there was a dramatic fall in CFC emissions in the Ukraine from 1989 to 1995, they started to rise again over the next seven years. In contrast, CFC emissions in Poland have fallen the most, from 5000 metric tons in 1989 to approximately 100 tons in 2002. Malaysia and Egypt are in the middle, showing steady declines in CFC emissions over the 13-year period. Looking at Malaysia in particular, CFC emissions remained stable from 1989 to 1995, but then fell sharply from 1995 to 2002.

In conclusion, I would say that the graph presents a generally positive picture for the world's environment, as the amount of CFC emissions has decreased a great deal.

7 Food and Diet

1 Introduction

Aims: To introduce the topic of food and diet and to act as lead-in to the reading.

To introduce some of the vocabulary which arises later in the unit.

To introduce the idea of agreeing and disagreeing with opinions.

To provide further practice in justifying opinions (introduced in earlier Speaking sections).

A
▸ Pre-teach *organic* and *GM* (genetically modified) *food*. (Organic food is grown without the use of chemicals, fertilisers and pesticides, GM food has been changed by genetic engineering.)
▸ Have students discuss the issues in pairs and then as a class. You could use the pictures at the top of the page to prompt discussion as to which food is healthy, why, and which type of food students would prefer to eat.

Extension: *Food alphabet race*

Aim: *To reinforce and review vocabulary related to food.*

Preparation
▸ Split the board in half and write the alphabet as a list down the left side of each half.

Procedure
▸ Put the students into 'teams' of 4–5.
▸ Set a time limit and explain that each team must write a food item for each letter.
▸ Check answers as a class, giving one point for each letter that students were able to think of a word for. You can offer extra points for words which no other team got, give half marks for incorrect spelling, etc.
▸ This activity can be used for vocabulary reinforcement of any lexical set.

B
▸ Put the students into groups of 5.
▸ Allocate one statement to each student in each group.
▸ Instruct the groups that they have to find out each student's response to their statement. They should not only find out if the student agrees or disagrees, but also why they have this opinion. Students will be asked to report back to the group on their findings. This should encourage students to justify their opinions.
▸ Have students give feedback as a mini-presentation.
▸ Provide students with simple structures such as:
The vast majority of ...
Just over half the group thought that ...
25% of the students ...
Most students ...
Only a few ...
Only one of ...

In the exam
Draw students' attention to the *In the exam* box. Point out how understanding opinion is a key exam skill. Explain briefly about the exam tasks, i.e. true/false/not given, yes/no/not given and completion tasks.

2 Identifying opinions

Aims: To provide practice in identifying the writer's opinion.

To clarify the difference between the yes/no/not given answers.

A
▸ Make sure students understand the statement clearly, teaching vocabulary as required. When students do the matching exercise, stress the difference between b and c: to answer 'no', the information in the statement has to have the opposite message to that presented in the text sentence. To answer 'not given', the information in the statement has to be completely new – not mentioned in the original text sentence.

B ▸ Explain the difference between the yes/no/not given questions in relation to the previous exercise: as before, students answer 'yes' or 'no', according to whether the statement agrees or disagrees with the original text sentence, and 'not given' if it is completely new information not mentioned in the original text sentence. Have students go on to answer yes/no/not given in relation to two further statements.

3 Yes/No/Not Given

Aim: To provide practice of yes/no/not given questions as a task type.

For this task
▸ Go through the *For this task* box, explaining the rubric of the task.
▸ As in previous tasks, you should draw attention to the importance of focusing on keywords and paraphrased information. Draw students' attention to the examples given.

Express tip
Read out the advice in this box while students follow in their books. It is always difficult for a student to know whether the answer is 'not given', or if it is actually 'yes' or 'no' and they have just missed the relevant section of text. Encourage students to assume that if they haven't found the information in the text after a reasonable period of time, they should select 'not given', instead of wasting a lot of time looking for it.

Exam practice
▸ Have students answer questions 1–8.

Support
▸ Pre-teach all or some of the following vocabulary items:
famine, overweight, health insurance, to ban something, junk food, a right to do something, rare, the cause of

something, persuade somebody to do something, responsibility for doing something, have an effect on something, interfere, someone's private business.

4 Summary completion

Aims: To introduce note-making as a lead-in to looking at the summary completion task.

To introduce summary completion as a task type.

A ▸ Ask students to recall the ideas in the text. Remind them that they did this in Unit 5, when they read about the invention of flight.
▸ Point out that their recollections have many details missing and that what they have in effect is a summary of the text.

B ▸ Have students put the notes in the correct order.

Express tip

Read out the advice in this box while students follow in their books. In a summary completion task such as this one, each missing item is worth one mark. Students should maximise the number of answers they get correct by leaving any difficult ones for now and answering the less difficult ones first if possible.

ANSWER KEY

The correct order is from left to right and top to bottom: 4, 3, 1, 2

For this task

▸ Students often find this IELTS task challenging and so it is worth spending some time going through the *For this task* box carefully.

▸ Draw students' attention to the information in the *For this task* box. Explain that there are two different types of summary completion task, and show them the differences between questions 9–15 and questions 16–19.

Support

▸ Explain how students should use both meaning and grammar to help them choose the correct word. In addition to the example presented here, you may like to do some supplementary work on parts of speech.

▸ Choose some sentences with unknown vocabulary and delete some keywords. Make sure you delete a variety of nouns, verbs, adjectives, adverbs, gerunds, infinitives, past participles, etc.
Ask the students first to decide on the part of speech, and only when they have done this to predict the missing word. E.g. *The professor was very .... in the field of criminology, he had .... all his life studying the psychological effects of ....*
The first gap must be an adjective, the second a past participle and the third a noun or gerund.

ANSWER KEY

knowledgeable; spent; prison

Exam practice
Questions 9–15

▸ Have students complete questions 9–15.
▸ Check answers as a class.

ANSWER KEY

9 Answer: agricultural productivity
Note 'Thanks to rising agricultural productivity, famine is rarer all over the globe.'

10 Answer: public-health
Note 'Obesity is the world's biggest public-health issue today ...'

11 Answer: safety and stability
Note 'Governments and people seem to agree that ensuring the safety and stability of the food supply is part of the state's job.'

12 Answer: behaviour
Note ' ... obesity is a more complicated issue ... it is about changing their behaviour.'

13 Answer: better eating habits
Note 'Governments should help guide them towards better eating habits. But that argument is weaker in the case of food than it is for tobacco ... '

14 Answer: (primary) school
Note 'The state ... should try to ensure that its small citizens aren't overdosing on sugar at primary school.'

15 Answer: comparable countries
Note 'Sweden already bans advertising to children, and its young people are as fat as those in comparable countries.'

Exam practice
Questions 16–19

▸ Have students complete questions 16–19.
▸ Check answers as a class.

ANSWER KEY

16 Answer: society
Note '... thin people subsidise fat people through health care.'

17 Answer: government
Note '... what should happen in a state-financed health system.'

18 Answer: levy
Note 'Why not tax fattening food ... '

19 Answer: freedom
Note '... intrusion on liberty ... But it also has a legitimate interest in not having the government interfere in people's private business.'

Section aims:
▶ To teach students a method to quickly generate ideas and develop critical thinking skills for Part 3 of the exam.
▶ To teach students to expand their answers to cover additional information related to the main points on the topic card in Part 2 of the exam, particularly when describing an experience.
▶ To provide further practice in Speaking Part 2: Individual long turn and Speaking Part 3: Two-way discussion.

1 Introduction

Aim: To introduce the topic of dining out and to elicit some of the vocabulary which arises later in the unit.

▶ Focus students' attention on the photo and ask questions to the class such as:
Do you think people eat together as a family less often than they used to?

What are some of the good and bad things about family dinners?

Try to develop the discussion by contrasting home-cooked family dinners with fast food restaurants. Possible questions might include:
Do you think people are eating more fast food and fewer meals at home with the family?

Do you think this is a good thing?

▶ Put students in pairs to ask and answer the discussion questions.
▶ As a follow-up task, focus students' attention on the photo and ask questions to the class which contrast the two different 'philosophies of food' – fast food or eating home cooked food with the family. Possible questions might include:
Why do people eat more fast food these days?

Do you think people eat together as a family less often?

What are some of the 'good' and 'bad' things about fast food meals?

The aim is to get students to 'see' and subsequently discuss the issues as represented by the two contrasting photos.

In the exam

Direct students' attention to the *In the exam* box and ask them to read through the information silently. Check their understanding by asking one or two questions, e.g.
What are you given in Part 2 of the exam?
How much time have you got to prepare?

2 Describing an experience

Aims: To practise visualisation techniques in preparation for speaking about a personal experience.

To provide further practice in taking notes in preparation for the 1–2 minute talk.

To get students to generate additional information they can include to expand on the main points on the card.

To expose students to a model candidate's performance which shows how additional information can be incorporated into a student's talk.

To present a format that students can use to describe information in a logical order – context, events, feelings.

A ▶ Have students read the information on the topic card, then close their eyes and visualise the situation. This activity works best when you create a calm, quiet atmosphere in the class – students should close their eyes and remember a recent restaurant experience. If your students find this activity difficult, you can help them by asking them to focus on different details – *How is the lighting in the restaurant? How are you dressed?* All the time, students will need to keep their eyes closed, concentrating on 'reliving' that moment.

B ▶ Explain to the class that you want them to write notes based on what they visualised, so they can use them in the next speaking activity.
▶ Demonstrate, using the board, what you want them to do. Write down notes answering the questions on the topic card based on your own experience.
▶ Have students prepare their own notes. Remind them to use note form, not full sentences, when noting down their thoughts. If they are unclear what is required, remind them to look back at the notes on page 30.

Express tip
Read out the advice in this box while students follow in their books. Remind them again that they only have a minute to take notes. The purpose of their notes is to act as a reminder of what to say, not to provide a script they can read out.

C 1

▸ Encourage students to 'get in touch' with what they remembered from the visualisation task in order to note down additional but relevant information.

ANSWER KEY
Other useful information could include:
why you went to that restaurant
what you did after the meal
what you thought about the price of the meal.

2

▸ Tell students they are going to listen to a model candidate giving a talk on the topic card. Give students a few seconds to look though the answers and check they understand what they need to do before playing the recording.
▸ Play recording 7.1 and have students complete the task.

ANSWER KEY
Points the student covered were: a, b, f, g, h

7.1 LISTENING SCRIPT ────────

Candidate: Well, the last time I ate at a restaurant was about two weeks ago, when I went to a fast food place in Oxford Street with my girlfriend. It was early in the evening, about six o'clock, and Oxford Street was very busy. It was also very wet because it was raining heavily ... and we didn't have an umbrella!
Anyway, I'm a vegetarian, so I had a veggie burger with French fries and a large chocolate milkshake which was SO good ... and only cost about £4. My girlfriend, Tomoko, had a salad and a bottle of mineral water because she doesn't like the type of food they have there. She didn't say anything but I don't think she liked the salad very much because it was covered in a very oily dressing. She was pretty angry by the end of the meal.

Express tip
Read out the advice in this box while students follow in their books. Throughout the rest of the lesson, encourage students to use these expressions when they are speaking.

3

▸ Tell students that when we give a talk, we need to present our thoughts in an organised fashion. Explain that when you describe an experience, it is very common to first 'describe the context, i.e. give background information to set the scene for the 'events'. The final part of this kind of talk might include some kind of reflection about the events that have taken time and this is a logical place to talk about 'feelings'.
▸ Play recording 7.1 again and ask students to do the exercise.

ANSWER KEY
context: a, b; events: f; feelings: h

Challenge
▸ Ask students what other information they could include in the three headings: Context, Events, Feelings. They can take information from C2 (a–e is Context, f and g Events, h Feelings), or come up with their own ideas. Possible examples include:
Context – description of the restaurant and some of the people there;
Events – describe anything unusual or surprising that happened, recount some elements of the conversation between you and your friend;
Feelings – contrast feelings expressed and feelings which are very real but not expressed, describe body language.

3 Individual long turn

Aim: To provide exam practice of Speaking Part 2.

For this task
▸ Put students into pairs and ask them to read through the *For this task* box before attempting the question.
▸ Tell student B that s/he should time student A for one (or possibly two) minutes – during this time, the 'examiner' should not interrupt, even if student A is silent and has nothing to say!

Exam practice

▸ After students have completed the task and swapped roles, you could ask one or two pairs of students who have performed well to role-play their talk to the rest of the class.

Express tip

Read out the advice in this box while students follow in their books. A minute can seem like a very long time if you are unprepared – stress to students that it will be much easier to speak for a minute if they use the minute beforehand to think about what they are going to say.

4 Generating ideas

Aims: To encourage students to develop critical thinking skills to help them analyse a question.

To introduce a technique that students can use to generate ideas to elaborate upon their answers in Speaking Part 3.

A ▸ Focus students' attention on the main question in the centre of the mind-map and tell them that a good way to generate ideas on any particular question is through using a technique known as the '5Ws and 1H', which will help them focus on different angles to the question.

▸ Write the question on the board and have students close their books.

▸ Elicit from students the five question words that start with W and the one that starts with H.

▸ Ask students to come up with questions (one for each of the question words 1H) that relate to the question on the board.

▸ Redirect students to the Coursebook and have them ask and answer the subsidiary questions in the mind-map together with any relevant questions they have generated themselves.

Note: Obviously, students will not have the time to go through this procedure in real time in the exam – the purpose of the exercise is to train students in critical thinking skills, so that when they do come to the exam they will be able to respond to questions with their own ideas, selecting different angles on the question. In effect, they will be changing a closed 'Yes/No question' to an open 'Wh question'.

▸ Students first discuss the question without the help of subsidiary wh questions (4A). Some students will have a lot to say and will consequently have dealt with some of the issues brought up in the subsidiary

questions in 4B. Other students will struggle with this type of question – not necessarily due to a lack of language, but rather a lack of ideas. In the latter case, the following exercise in 4B will be invaluable in extending answers and getting students to think around the question.

B ▸ Have students work in pairs. Ask each pair to discuss together the six questions in the mind-map.

▸ When all pairs have finished, elicit answers to the six questions from the class.

Express tip

Read out the advice in this box while students follow in their books. It is very unlikely that students will have time in the exam to think of answers to all these questions. By practicing the technique in class they can make the procedure 'automatic'.

C As a class, brainstorm some 'Why' questions and write *Why is fast food bad for children? Why are many people concerned about advertising fast food to children?* on the board to provide a model question and initiate discussion on some of the possible angles to take with this question.

ANSWER KEY

Example questions

Who is worried about fast food companies advertising to children?

What kind of advertising might be acceptable?

Why should fast food companies limit their advertising to children?

Where should fast food companies be able to freely advertise?

When should fast food companies not advertise on TV?

How should advertising be controlled?

---

5 Two-way discussion

Aim: To provide exam practice of Speaking Part 3.

For this task

▸ Have students read the *For this task* box and answer any queries they may have.

▸ Put the students into pairs and make clear that one student in each pair is Student A and the other is Student B. Check, by calling on random students, that everyone knows which they are. Explain that students will hear questions on the recording and will have to answer the questions to their partner, when you pause the recording.

Student A

▸ Play recording 7.2 and have students answer questions 1–3. Encourage student B to take notes on student A's performance. Student B is in effect playing the role of examiner.

▸ Have student B give feedback to student A, using his or her notes for details.

7.2 LISTENING SCRIPT ──────────────

Student A

1 How would you define a healthy diet?

2 What do you think are the reasons why many people do not eat healthy food?

3 How can governments encourage people to eat more healthily?

Student B

▸ Swap roles for questions 4–6 to give both students an opportunity to practise.

▸ Play recording 7.3 and have students answer questions 4–6.

7.3 LISTENING SCRIPT ──────────────

Student B

4 Are fast food companies responsible for making people fat?

5 Why do you think fast food is so popular?

6 What would happen if restaurants had to label all their meals to clearly show ingredients, calories, fat content, etc.?

IELTS Express Speaking Video

If you are using the *Speaking Video* which accompanies *IELTS Express*, Sections 3 and 4 of the video relate to the content of this unit. If you haven't already shown these videos to your class, they could be shown at the beginning of this lesson, to give students a recap of the content and format of the Parts 2 and 3 of the IELTS Speaking exam.

At the end of the lesson, you should show your class Section 5 of the video, which contains a full model IELTS interview. This will help review everything which has been taught in the course and give students an idea of what to expect in the exam.

For more information on the *IELTS Express Speaking Video DVD* and how to integrate it into your lessons, see page 103.

8 Sickness and Health

> **Section aims:**
> ▸ To introduce and practise the skill of understanding a description of an illustration or plan.
> ▸ To practise identifying differences between pictures.
> ▸ To introduce and to provide practice in Listening Section 4: Academic monologue.
> ▸ To practise a number or task types: labelling a diagram, multiple-choice with multiple answers, multiple-choice with pictures.

1 Introduction

Aim: To introduce the topic of sickness and health and to introduce some of the topic-related vocabulary which arises later in the unit.

A ▸ On the board, write *heart, lungs, liver, thumb* and *Which is the odd one out?*

▸ Elicit the answer 'thumb' and ask why. Explain that 'thumb' is the only one that is not an internal organ, and so it is the odd one out.

▸ Ask students to work in pairs and find the odd one out in lists 1–5.

▸ When you are checking answers, ask why a particular word is the odd one out. Drill the pronunciation and stress of each word.

Support

▸ Depending on the nationality of your students and the existence of cognates in their own language, this exercise may present a few difficulties. Speakers of non-Romance languages (e.g. Asian) could use their dictionaries. You could turn this exercise into a race, the winning pair being the first group to bring you all five correct answers.

> **ANSWER KEY**
> 1 treatment: This is a process, the others are all physical or notional parts of a hospital.
> 2 surgery: This is a medical process, the others are all people.
> 3 cure: this is what makes you better. The others are what make you ill.
> 4 administration: This deals with running the hospital, the others are all areas of specialisation in medicine.
> 5 architecture: This is the study of building design, the others are all units within a hospital.

B ▸ You could suggest that students construct a bubble diagram. Put the word 'hospital' in the middle and radiating branches labelled *people, rooms,*

departments, etc. Collect all ideas together and put them in one big diagram on the board.

> **ANSWER KEY**
> **Possible answers are:**
> **People:** surgeon, porter, physician, physiotherapist, etc.;
> **rooms:** maternity ward, operating theatre, waiting room, examination room, etc.;
> **departments:** Oncology, Accident and Emergency, Cardiology, etc.

In the exam

Direct students' attention to the *In the exam* box and ask them to read through the information silently. Check their understanding by asking one or two questions, e.g. *What do you listen to in Part 4 of the Listening exam? What kinds of task types are mentioned here?*

2 Understanding description

Aims: To introduce vocabulary used to describe position.

To introduce and practise the skill of labelling a diagram.

A ▸ Tell students they will now practise labelling a diagram.

▸ Students work in pairs. Ask them to look at the diagram of a hospital on page 65 of the Coursebook and describe what they see to their partner. Encourage them to use the words in the box in their descriptions. Though not all the buildings are labelled, encourage them to try to identify them using the numbers, e.g. building number 2 is behind building number 1, on the right.

▸ Have the students look at the labels. Ask them how they are numbered. At this point, you could teach: *horizontal(ly), vertical(ly), from top to bottom, from bottom to top, from left to right, clockwise, anti-clockwise.*

- Ask them to discuss the difference between Questions 1–5 and Questions 6–10 with their partner, before opening it up to the class.
- Encourage your students to say the words in the box of answers to themselves. If the class has difficulty with pronunciation of any of the items, have students chorally repeat the vocabulary as a class.

ANSWER KEY

Possible answers:

1 Building number 1 is at the bottom of the diagram. Behind it there are two rows of buildings with one big building at the end and a small building in the middle of the rows. Building number 6 is to the left of numbers 3 and 4.

2 Labels 1–5 are numbered vertically, bottom to top. Labels 6–10 are labelled horizontally, from left to right (or clockwise).

3 Questions 1–5 are matching questions, questions 6–10 are label completion questions. You could explain that matching questions are similar to classification questions, which were covered in Unit 6 Listening. The only difference is that each answer can only be used once, and that students will not need to use all the possible answers.

Express tip

Read out the advice in this box while students follow in their books.

B
- Play recording 8.1. Remind students they only have to write the code, not the full answer.

Challenge
- With stronger groups, play the first part of the recording all the way through.

Support
- With weaker groups, you could stop the recording after each answer, replaying the relevant part of the recording if most are having problems.

ANSWER KEY

1 AB; 2 ICU; 3 OGU; 4 L; 5 FM

8.1 LISTENING SCRIPT

In today's Architecture & Society lecture, we look at hospital design. Now, one of the first modern hospitals was the Hospital de Sant Pau in Barcelona, Spain, which was designed by the Catalan architect Domenech I Montaner and completed in 1930. As you can see, the hospital is built on a large, square site, surrounded by a

wall. The buildings are laid out on the diagonal. The main entrance is in one corner, at the bottom of the plan here. You enter through this large building, which is also the main Administration Block. Behind this are two parallel rows of smaller buildings, or pavilions, each dedicated to a separate function. For example, the first on the right is the Intensive Care Unit. Opposite that is the building for Digestive Disorders. The third building on the left is the Obstetrics and Gynaecology Unit, for the treatment of women's health care. After that, also on the left, are the laboratories. At the end of this avenue of pavilions is a large building with two wings. This is the Faculty of Medicine and incorporates the Blood Bank and Radiography Unit.

C
- Remind students about identifying the question, underlining the keywords, thinking about synonyms or paraphrases and identifying the answer type. If necessary, refer them back to the Listening sections in Units 2 and 4 to revise these skills. Let them work through stages 1–3 of preparation for each question. You could do the first couple as a group, then let them do the rest in pairs.

ANSWER KEY

6 The question is: 'Who (or What) is treated in the Psychiatric block?' The answer is a disease, disorder or maybe definition of a type of patient.

7 The question is: 'What is stored in the building in the middle of the top left hand wall?' A paraphrase is: 'What is kept … the centre … ?' The answer is an object or objects.

8 The question is: 'What is the name of the block where major operations take place?' The answer is a name.

9 The question is: 'Who (or What) is treated in the Paediatric block?' The answer is a disease, disorder or maybe definition of a type of patient.

10 The question is: 'The building in the right hand corner is called the House of what?' A paraphrase is 'on the far right'. The answer is a name or function.

D
- Play recording 8.2. Students now answer questions 6–10.
- **Architectural Note**

If your students are interested, you can explain the radical approach to the design of this hospital a little further:

In 1900, Barcelona's healthcare facilities were in crisis. The only existing hospital was four hundred years old, as were its drains and services. It was so unsanitary that a patient's chances of recovery probably dropped as they entered its front door. It was clear that a new hospital was needed and the Catalan architect Domenech I Montaner was given the job of designing it.

Previously, there had been two basic approaches to hospital design: the monoblock and the polyblock. The monoblock approach consisted of one big building with everything under one roof. The problem here was that it was impossible for patients to recover if they shared the same space as patients with infectious diseases. The polyblock approach set out to solve this problem by separating patients in different buildings. This approach created a new problem – that of moving patients, or sensitive medical equipment and supplies, from one block to another without exposing them to the elements.

Domenech came up with a brilliant solution. He excavated the whole site and built all the hospital's service areas and corridors underground. On top of this he built a series of 48 buildings or pavilions, each linked to the service net through their basements. Each pavilion had a specific function. Gardens and trees were planted between each pavilion and the whole place has the feel of a village.

The Hospital de Sant Pau was awarded UNESCO World Heritage status in 1997.

Challenge

▸ With stronger groups, play the recording all the way through.

Support

▸ With weaker groups, you could stop the recording after each answer, replaying the relevant part of the recording if most are having problems.

ANSWER KEY

6 mental problems

7 (medical) records

8 surgery

9 babies and children

10 recovery

8.2 **LISTENING SCRIPT**

Around this central avenue are other buildings. On the left, in the middle, we find the Psychiatric Block, where patients with mental problems are treated. Now, Domenech had great attention to detail, he even created a house specifically for storing medical records. It's that small building there, near the centre of the wall on the left.

Moving round, we come to this long building, which dominates this part of the site. This is the Surgery Block, where most of the major operations take place. Moving round again, the building to the right of the avenue is the Paediatrics Unit. This is where babies and children receive treatment. Finally, in this right hand corner we have the 'Casa de Convalecencia' or House of Recovery. This was where you stayed if you were not confined to bed, but were still not quite well enough to go home. These days it is not part of the hospital, but is used by a university language department.

Domenech's radical approach to hospital design was a major step forward in health care, but what else have architects done to improve our health?

Extension: *Labelling a floor plan*

Aim: *To provide additional practice in labelling a diagram.*

Preparation

▸ Students will need to draw a plan or a room in their house. Drawing and labelling the diagrams in this activity may be time consuming in class. You might prefer to have students do it for homework before the next class.

Procedure

▸ Ask students to draw a plan of a room in their house, or maybe a floor plan of another building which they know well, but their partner does not, and partially label it.

▸ Ask them to write a description of this diagram or plan.

▸ Each student should give the unfinished plan to their partner and then read out their descriptions while their partners complete the labels.

▸ With more advanced classes, the students could dictate the directions to their partner and have him or her draw the floor plan based on their description.

3 Identifying differences between pictures

Aim: To introduce students to multiple-choice questions in which the answer is given in the form of a picture.

A
▸ Ask students to work in pairs. Tell them to look at the four pictures at the top of page 66. Ask them to tell their partner what the pictures have in common.

▸ Ask them to describe to their partner the most important difference between each picture, possibly even writing it down.

▸ Have students identify the keyword for each difference and consider any synonyms or paraphrasing.

ANSWER KEY

1 They all show a man who has been injured in some way.

2 The pictures show:
  A a man with a broken <u>right arm</u>
  B a man with a broken <u>right leg</u> on <u>crutches</u>
  C a man with a broken <u>left arm</u>
  D a man with a broken <u>right leg</u> in a <u>wheelchair</u>.

3 Keywords underlined above.

B
▸ Ask students to read the instructions carefully, identify the keywords in the question and consider any synonyms.

▸ Play recording 8.3 and have students answer Question 1.

▸ Check the answer as a class.

ANSWER KEY

1 B

8.3 LISTENING SCRIPT ————————

But I'm pleased to report that no fatalities occurred in the accident. The schoolchildren only suffered minor injuries – cuts and bruises – and the bus driver, who sustained <u>a compound fracture of the patella of his right leg, is now up and about – though he still needs support to walk</u>.

4 Labelling a diagram

Aims: To introduce labelling a diagram as a task type.

To provide further practice in Listening Section 4.

For this task

▸ Ask students to read through the *For this task* box, highlighting the keywords.

▸ After they finish, ask them to close their books and tell their partner how they would attempt the task.

Exam practice
Questions 1–6

▸ Play recording 8.4 and have students complete the task.

▸ Have students check answers with each other and then with you.

Challenge

▸ With stronger groups, play the recording straight away, straight through.

Support

With weaker groups, work through the stages of the process for Questions 1–5. Then play recording 8.4.

ANSWER KEY

1 windpipe	4 remove waste
2 oxygen	5 (kind of) bag
3 nutrients (from food)	

8.4 LISTENING SCRIPT ————————

Good afternoon, ladies and gentlemen. Welcome to Medical School. First, let us remind ourselves of the reason we are all here – the human body.

The human body survives on air, food and water. These are processed by several organs, which are all located in the main, central part of the body, which is known as the torso. Today we've only got a <u>plastic model of a human torso</u>. You'll have to wait a while before we let you get your hands on the real thing!

OK, let's look how this thing works. Air enters the body through the mouth and nose and is carried to the lungs through the trachea, <u>commonly known as the windpipe</u>. The lungs – and there are two of them, one on the left, one on the right – <u>take oxygen from the air and put it into the blood</u>. This oxygen-carrying blood is then pumped around the body by the heart, via a series of tubes known as arteries and veins. Please note the location of the heart. It is in the centre of the chest, not on the left as we often imagine!

Now, in the lower part of the torso, the abdomen, we find a series of long tubes. These are your intestines, and again you have two of them: a small intestine and a large intestine. The job of the intestine is to absorb nutrients from food you have eaten earlier and collect waste material before it is excreted. It usually takes food about 24 hours to pass through the intestine.

Above the intestine is the liver. The liver is a large organ and has the important job of separating toxic from useful substances. The kidneys remove waste and pass it into the urine. The kidneys are located behind the intestine – and I think you can just see them at the back at either side there. Down at the bottom here, we have the bladder, a kind of bag where urine is collected. This bladder is emptied of urine when we urinate.

OK. Any questions so far?

5 Multiple-choice (pictures); multiple-choice with multiple answers

Aim: To introduce multiple-choice with pictures and multiple-choice with multiple answers as task types.

For this task

Read through the *For this task* box with your students. When they have finished, ask them to close their books and tell their partner what they can remember.

Exam practice

Questions 1–2

▶ As this is the final listening in the core of this book, do not help students too much.

▶ Play recording 8.5 and have students answer the questions.

▶ Check the answers. Ask students to describe the position of the body in each picture and play the recording again.

ANSWER KEY

1 c; 2 a

8.5 LISTENING SCRIPT

Now, let's look at some basic emergency procedures. First, fainting. Someone has fainted and they are lying flat out on the floor. What's the first thing to do? Answer: If necessary, roll them over so they are lying on their back. Raise both their feet above the level of the head. Why? To increase the blood circulation to the brain. Secondly, make sure their breathing passage is clear. Do this by turning the head to one side and tilting it back. If the fainting attack lasts for more than a few seconds, place the person in the recovery position, which is done like this ...

Exam practice

Questions 3–4

▶ Don't give students any support, just play the recording and check the answers. When checking the answers, refer to the listening script and/or play the recording again. Ask students if any of the other options are mentioned (they are). Tell them that the examiner will often include reference to the incorrect options and this is why students should be careful not to choose an option as the answer just because they hear it.

▶ Play recording 8.6 and have students answer the questions.

ANSWER KEY

3,4 A, E (in either order)

8.6 LISTENING SCRIPT

While I remember ... As medical students, you'll be regularly visiting – and working in – hospital wards. Now, you will be expected to wear a white coat. If you don't have one, you'd better get one.

I also strongly suggest you buy yourself the following items: A notebook. You are going to be getting an awful lot of information thrown at you over the next few years. Make sure you keep good notes. Obviously, you'll be needing a pen. A thermometer is always useful for taking a patient's temperature, as is a watch for checking their pulse. Please don't bring your mobile phone with you, as they can interfere with some of the equipment. Finally, if you haven't bought your own stethoscope just yet, don't worry – the department will supply you with these. One last thing. Please don't drive to the hospital, you will certainly find it impossible to park anywhere nearby. One or two students have tried to park in the ambulance bays and have got into all sorts of trouble. Please use public transport.

Section aims:
▸ To provide students with an alternative approach to writing 'agree or disagree' essays from that given in Unit 4.
▸ To provide practice in brainstorming arguments 'for' and 'against' and using these arguments to support statements and opinions.
▸ To show students a way of structuring an 'agree or disagree' essay.
▸ To provide further practice with General Training Task 2.

1 Introduction

Aim: To introduce health-related vocabulary that students can use in the Exam practice section at the end of the unit.

A ▸ Focus students' attention on the photos and ask them *What do these photos show?* Elicit from the students that the photos contrast healthy and unhealthy lifestyles. Follow this up by brainstorming other examples of healthy and unhealthy lifestyles and put up vocabulary on the board: **healthy:** *going to the gym, doing sport, living in the country;* **unhealthy:** *long hours in front of the TV, fast food, living in the city.*

▸ Explain the meaning of prevention, cure and illneses and ask students to do the exercise in pairs. With reference to the photos, ask students what illness you can get from smoking (lung cancer, bronchitis), and what the cure for these illnesses might be (stop smoking, therapy for cancer). Finally, ask students how these diseases could be prevented in the first place (never start smoking!). Don't answer any other vocabulary questions at this stage – this can be checked at the end of the task.

> **ANSWER KEY**
>
> **Illness and cures:** take medicine, take antibiotics, undergo surgery, die of cancer, get/have HIV/AIDS, get/have flu;
>
> **Health prevention:** stop smoking, take up sport, reduce stress, be a positive thinker, eat a balanced diet, sleep well, get a vaccination

B ▸ Ask students for additional vocabulary they might have for the three categories: *illness, prevention, cure* and write any items they come up with on the board – you might have to feed in extra vocabulary and ideas at this stage, e.g. **prevention:** *walk to work, get off the bus one stop before your stop, take the stairs not the lift;* **cure:** *rest, holiday, friends, laughter, homeopathic remedies;* **illness:** *depression, a cold, food poisoning.*

In the exam

Draw students' attention to the *In the exam* box. Have students read through the information silently and then ask questions to check their understanding of the key points of the exam in relation to Writing Task 2. Example questions might include:
What is the difference between a 'for and against' essay and an 'agree or disagree' essay?
Is there a choice of questions?

2 Supporting your statements and opinions

Aims: To encourage students to support statements and opinions using appropriate linking words.

To provide an opportunity for students to offer their own ideas and opinions.

A ▸ Emphasise to students that opinion and statements by themselves are not academically valid, as they are unsupported and unsubstantiated, and consequently they will be marked down in the exam. Examples of unsupported and unsubstantiated statements are found in the five sentences in the exercise – they need to be extended to be supported and substantiated.

▸ Point out to students the linking words *because, as, since,* which are used to support and justify opinions and statements.

B ▸ This exercise is more difficult than the preceding one, as students will need to come up with the language and the ideas to complete the sentences. Allow students to use dictionaries. If the class is having difficulty, ask prompt questions to elicit answers.

3 Brainstorming arguments for and against

Aims: To present students with an exam question and get them to take a position – agree or disagree.

To encourage students to think more deeply about why they agree or disagree and to come up with arguments to support their position.

To generate discussion and hopefully disagreement between students regarding a controversial issue.

A ▸ Check students understand the question and have them decide whether they agree or disagree with the statement.

B ▸ Have students circle if they agree or disagree with the sentence in the box, then list arguments to support their position. It's not necessary for students to write full sentences – note form will do.

C ▸ Have students compare and discuss their answers with a partner. Encourage discussion and disagreement here – circulate and play 'devil's advocate'. As a class, call on individual students to offer some of the arguments they've provided.

Extension: *Smoking debate*

Aim: *To provide further practice in developing arguments for and against a position, in the context of a debate.*

Procedure
▸ Set up a formal debate by dividing the class into two camps – 'smokers' and 'non-smokers' and separate them in two different sides of the classroom. This has the effect of setting up an adversarial situation which reflects the nature of 'agree or disagree' questions. The two groups should be roughly equal in number, so if you don't have

enough smokers in the class, select some non-smokers to role-play as smokers.

▸ Give students 5 minutes to compare their notes in their two groups, to build their case for or against the exam question in section 3A. If students don't have much to say, then circulate between the two groups playing devil's advocate – taking the opposite opinion to what students are saying to stimulate discussion. Be controversial!

▸ When they are ready, select or have each group select one or more speakers from each side to put forward the arguments.

▸ After the speeches, open up the debate to questions. Take a vote at the end as a class to determine which side won.

4 Structuring an 'agree or disagree' essay

Aim: To present contrasting model essays which teach students how to express and organise their ideas, whichever position they take on the question – agree or disagree.

A ▸ Remind students to use the skimming techniques they have practised in the Reading sections to do these two tasks.

B ▸ In discussing the essays in pairs or small groups, encourage students to engage personally with the essays – which one do they agree with more? What extra points were made in the essays that the students had not thought of in the preceding exercises? Which essay is more convincing (on an objective level)?

C ▸ After checking through the answers, finish off by asking students *Which essay did you find more convincing on an objective level?* Try to get students to respond on the basis of what arguments were most convincing, irrespective of their personal viewpoint. There are no right or wrong answers here.

D
> Split the class in two and ask one half to do the exercise in relation to essay 1 and the other half to do it with essay 2.

> To start with, go through a model answer with students as a class. Take the first highlighted phrase in essay 2 and ask students which of the six essay writing features it is. If students get this wrong, explain why it is wrong and ask them to guess again.

> Have students do the exercise and then compare their answers for essay 1 and essay 2.

Extension 1: *Open questions*

Aim: The use of open questions to support a position might be new to students and so more time might usefully be set aside to give more practice in using this technique.

Procedure

> Write on the board additional open questions which support a particular position, e.g. *Is it surprising that people who eat fast food every day suffer from obesity?* Ask students what the obvious answer to the question is and then ask them what position the question takes: *Is this open question for or against fast food?*

> Follow up by asking them to create an open question in favour of fast food, e.g. *Is it right to close down fast food restaurants if millions of people want to eat in them?*

Extension 2: *Language and stylistic features*

Aim: To draw students attention to other language and stylistic features in the essay.

Procedure

> Draw students' attention to the following stylistic techniques in the essays and ask them to identify examples.

1 Punctuation to emphasise a strongly held opinion. An example occurs in essay 1, paragraph D.

2 The use of a short sentence to maximise impact. Examples occur in Essay 2, paragraphs B and C.

3 Punctuation to indicate words used by someone else, and to indicate that you think differently. An example appears in Essay 2, Paragraph B.

5 Academic and General Training: Essay

Aims: To give students the opportunity to consolidate the skills introduced in this unit.

To practise a complete Task 2 essay.

To practise writing within a specified time limit.

For this task

> Have students work together to cover the points set out in the *For this task* box. Ask them to read these as preparation for the exam practice. Like previous *For this task* information boxes, this box provides students with a summary of the skills they have learnt within this section. Remind your students that you expect them to apply these points to their essay writing in the exam practice!

Exam practice

> Either set this for homework or, alternatively, do it in class as a timed essay.

Model answer

I very much agree with the statement that governments are not spending their health budgets in the best possible way. If governments continue to spend such large sums of money on treating illness and disease instead of preventing these diseases, then perhaps they should rename our national health services 'national illness services'!

Governments will probably argue that it is necessary to spend a large proportion of health budgets on treating illness because the general population do not live healthy lifestyles and so become ill. They would argue that most people do not listen to health campaigns. Also, they would say it is not possible to prevent many illnesses and diseases such as flu and many types of cancer, as well as accidents and emergencies. The problem with this argument is that it is very negative because it assumes that people are stupid and refuse to lead healthy lives. However, when people have the right information, they often do the right thing – in my country (Sweden), people now smoke and drink a lot less than in the past. I believe that the main reason for this is government health campaigns, including very strong health warnings on the products.

In my opinion, governments can do a lot to prevent not only illnesses and disease, but also accidents. Why don't governments spend more money on installing speed cameras on roads to make people drive more slowly? That would reduce the number of accidents.

To summarise, I really think that there is a lot that governments can do to prevent illness and disease to make the world a healthier place to live. In particular, rich governments can spend more money on scientific research to find the causes of new diseases such as AIDS, while governments from less well-developed countries can spend money on providing clean water for all their people. In this way, the world will have less need for expensive cures and hospitals.

An Introduction to Letter Writing

1A

Section aims:
▸ To prepare students for the different types of letters that they can encounter in the exam.
▸ To teach students how to use different registers, set phrases and an appropriate format in formal, semi-formal and informal letters.
▸ To teach students how to plan and structure their letters, following the three bullet points in the exam question.
▸ To introduce and provide practice with Task 1 of the IELTS General Training Writing module.

1 Introduction

Aim: To introduce the topic of letter writing as a lead-in to Task 1 of the General Training Writing module.

▸ Ask one or two of the questions to the students as a class and then put students in pairs to continue.

In the Exam

Draw students' attention to the *In the exam* box. As this is the first time students are seeing a unit that is exclusively a General Training (GT) unit, it is a good idea to briefly introduce this part of the exam before launching into the exercises. You can remind students that there is a full description of the GT paper in the *Introduction to the exam* at the beginning of the Coursebook.

Ask questions to test students' comprehension.

How is the General Training module different from the Academic Training module?

How many words do students need to write in Writing Task 1?

Is there a choice of questions in the Writing exam?, etc.

2 Recognising types of letters

Aims: To introduce students to different types of letters that frequently occur in the exam, by providing practice in identifying the purpose of letters from their first paragraphs.

To provide set phrases to open and end letters, based on the level of formality and the purpose of the letter.

To enable students to identify the level of formality that will be required in a letter, by identifying the relationships between the sender and the recipient.

A ▸ Explain that the five yellow boxes are the opening paragraphs of five letters and ask the students to read them.

Express tip

Read out the advice in this box while students follow in their books. Explain that while it is fine to use contractions in informal and semi-formal letters, they can sound too casual in formal letters.

B ▸ Check that students understand the vocabulary in the instructions (*complaint, request a favour,* etc) before you ask them to match the five openings (1–5) to the five purposes.
▸ Check answers as a class. Elicit the phrase in each opening that indicates what the purpose of the letter is.

ANSWER KEY

1 requesting information *'I am writing to enquire about ...'*

2 requesting a favour *'Can you let me have ...?'*

3 making a complaint *'I am writing to complain about ...'*

4 explaining a situation *'I am writing to let you know ...'*

5 introducing yourself *'I'm writing to tell you a little bit about myself.'*

C ▸ Have students discuss with a partner the relationship between the writer and the recipient in each letter. Ask them to decide whether each letter is formal, semi-formal or informal.

ANSWER KEY

1 prospective student to school administration (formal)

2 classmate to classmate (informal)

3 customer to bank manager (formal)

4 student to school administration (formal)

5 student to host family (semi-formal)

Express tip

Read out the advice in this box while students follow in their books. This information will help them identify which letter endings are appropriate to the opening sentences in the next exercise.

D ▸ Check that students understand the instructions and then ask them to match the endings to the beginnings of the five letters.

> **ANSWER KEY**
>
> 1 a; 2 c; 3 e; 4 b; 5 d
>
> **Note:** Students may have difficulty distinguishing closings **a** and **e**. In this case, point out that *Yours faithfully* in **a** matches with *Dear Sir/Madam* in **1**, while *Yours sincerely* in **e** matches with *Dear Mr. White* in **3**.

3 Planning a letter

Aims: To provide an opportunity to apply the skills and knowledge introduced in the previous section to analyse an exam practice question.

To provide students with a technique for generating appropriate ideas that they can include in their answer to an exam, and to assist students in being able to distinguish relevant from irrelevant information to include in an answer.

To show students how to organise ideas according to the bullet points in the question.

A ▸ Have students read the exam question and answer the three questions. They should not answer the exam question at this point.

> **ANSWER KEY**
>
> **The main purpose** is to request a loan; the **relationship** is customer to bank manager; the **level of formality required** is formal.

B ▸ Ask students to read through the exam question again. Encourage them to visualise the situation and imagine they are talking to the bank manager. What would they say? Emphasise that they need to be convincing to get what they want!

Express tip

Read out the advice in this box while students follow in their books. Explain that in all Task 1 letters, students are expected to use their imagination to supply supporting information for their letters.

C ▸ Remind students that the ideas and information they include in their letter must be relevant to the exam question. Have them read through the seven points and choose the five that are most relevant. Students can complete the task individually or in pairs. If students' answers differ from the answer key, then ask them to explain why they think the point they have included is relevant.

> **ANSWER KEY**
>
> **Relevant points:** 1, 4, 5, 6, 7

D ▸ Ask students to decide which of the points they identified in 3C match the points a–c in the exam question.

> **ANSWER KEY**
>
> a 1, 6; b 4, 5; c 7

E ▸ Remind students of the visualisation task they did in 3B and have them note down their answers. Explain that using note form rather than full sentences is much faster. They should omit articles and prepositions.

F ▸ Have students use their notes from the previous exercise to write full sentences, taking care to produce grammatically correct sentences.

4 Using appropriate language and organisation

Aims: To introduce students to the organisation and punctuation conventions of a formal or semi-formal letter.

To demonstrate the use of vocabulary to express a formal register.

To provide a model answer to an IELTS exam question.

A ▸ Read the rubric here aloud to the class. Explain this three-part structure and answer any questions about it.

▸ Have students read the letter alone, and then discuss the two questions with a partner. (The answer to both these questions is 'yes'). Some good students may notice that the closing of this letter, 'best wishes', is of the wrong register. This is a deliberate error which will be picked up on in the next section. If students don't notice this, don't point it out.

Express tip

Read out the advice in this box while students follow in their books. Students will have an opportunity to practice this tip in Section 5 of this unit.

B ▸ Explain to students that although they do not need to write addresses in an IELTS letter, it needs to be set out properly. Presentation is important – 'it's not just what you say, it's how you say it'. For example, running two paragraphs together without leaving a blank line between them can confuse the reader, who may see them as a single long paragraph.

▸ Have students read the letter again and identify which guideline of the six here has not been followed.

Challenge

▸ Tell students that sometimes (but not often) they are required to write an informal letter to a friend. Ask students to tell you which of the six guidelines would not apply to a letter to a friend (for the purposes of IELTS). The answer is 4 – the letter would be signed with only the first name.

C ▸ Explain again the importance of register and emphasise that writing in any language tends to be more formal than the spoken form. Use question 1 as an example.

▸ Have students look through the text for another way of saying 'I want to ask for' and elicit the answer from the class – 'I would like to request ...'

▸ Have students complete the exercise alone and then check their answers with a partner.

5 General Training Writing Task 1: Letter

Aims: To give students the opportunity to consolidate the skills introduced in this unit.

To practise a complete GT Task 1 Writing activity.

To practise writing within a specified time limit.

For this task

▸ Have students read silently through the *For this task* box for a summary of points they need to keep in mind when writing a GT Task 1 letter.

▸ After students have read through the points, ask them to close their books and tell you in their own words what the points are. Have students refer back to 2 to review letter openings and closings.

Exam practice

▸ Either set the exam question for homework or do it in class. Depending on the level of the class, you could extend the time limit from 20 to 30 minutes, as this is the first time students will have seen and done a Task 1 Writing question.

Model answer

Dear Sir/Madam,

My name is Renata Pereira from Sao Paolo in Brazil. I have recently registered as a student at your college to follow a four-week course in Advanced Computer Programming starting at the end of November this year.

I am writing to you to try to decide on my accommodation while I'm in Manchester. Ideally, I would like to stay with a host family because I think that this will also help me to improve my English. If possible, I would like to stay very close to the College so I don't need to spend a lot of time travelling. Last year, I studied on a Business English course in San Diego, USA and stayed with a host family and really enjoyed it very much. I am hoping for the same experience in Manchester.

I'd really appreciate it if you could send me any information you have regarding the different accommodation options (particularly host families). In particular, I'd like to know where the accommodation is and how much it costs.

I look forward to hearing from you soon.

Yours faithfully,

Renata Pereira

Writing a Letter of Complaint

1B

Section aims:
- To teach visualisation and role play techniques as a way of generating appropriate ideas and content for exam answers.
- To teach a range of time expressions to recount past events as they relate to letters of complaint and letters of explanation.
- To teach students how to use reported speech as a way of providing evidence to support their complaints.
- To give further practice in Task 1 of the IELTS General Training Writing module, with specific reference to letters of complaint.

1 Introduction

Aim: To introduce the topic of complaining, in particular, writing a letter of complaint.

- Have students read along with the text as you read the questions aloud. Elicit answers from one or two students as a class.
- Put students in pairs or small groups to discuss their experiences and have them answer the questions together.

In the exam

Draw students' attention to the *In the exam* box. Explain that their letters will be assessed according to the same criteria as the Academic Writing module. For a description of these criteria, have them read the *In the exam* box on page 36 of the coursebook.

2 Beginning a letter of complaint

Aim: To provide students with model opening paragraphs to different letters of complaint, including ways to express the degree of the writer's dissatisfaction.

A ‣ Explain to the class that the three yellow boxes contain the first sentences of three letters. Have students match the letters to the three complaints.

ANSWER KEY

1 a hotel room; **2** a travel delay; **3** hotel staff

Express tip

Read out the advice in this box while students follow in their books. The expressions in bold are suitable for any formal letter of complaint.

B ‣ Ask students to match the letters to the three businesses listed.

ANSWER KEY

1 package holiday company; **2** airline; **3** hotel

C ‣ **1** Have students discuss the questions here in pairs.
‣ **2** After checking the answer as a class, have students memorise the three set phrases in bold – give them 30 seconds to memorise, then ask them to close their books and rewrite the sentences. Ask three students to write up the sentences on the board and have the class tell you whether they are correct or not.

ANSWER KEY

Letter 2; 'I am writing to express my total dissatisfaction and frustration with ...'

3 Imagining the situation

Aims: To analyse an exam practice question in preparation for generating ideas to answer the question.

To have students imagine and then role play a scene, as a technique for generating ideas for their letters.

A ‣ Explain to the class that the section in bold type is a sample exam question. Draw students' attention to the two bulleted questions and ask them to discuss them in pairs.

ANSWER KEY

The purpose of the letter is to complain about a lack of heating and hot water. The relationship is tenant to landlord.

B ▸ Explain to the class that they are going to practice a visualisation activity to help them come up with ideas for their answers to this exam question. Have them close their eyes for one minute as you talk them through their visualisation. Explain that they don't need to write anything at this stage. Ask the following questions which they should answer in their own heads.

You are sitting in your flat now in London – How are you feeling?

It's winter, what can you see out of the window? How does it feel inside the flat?

How are you dressed? What does your flat look like?

When was the last time you took a bath?

How are you feeling right now about your landlord? What would you like to say to him if you speak to him now?

▸ After students have visualised the scene silently, put them into pairs to roleplay a telephone conversation with the landlord. Direct students' attention to the four points that they need to cover in their conversation. After students have completed the role-play, put them into different pairs and have them change roles and repeat.

Express tip

Read out the advice in this box while students follow in their books. Visualising the situation in this way, for a minute or two before they begin writing in the exam, will help students use their imagination to produce examples to support their arguments.

C ▸ After doing the roleplays, have students note down some of the language that the 'tenant' used in the roleplay. Elicit a few examples from the class and write them on the board.

4 Describing past events

Aims: To provide a model answer letter for the exam practice question previously discussed.

To introduce a variety of useful time expressions for describing a sequence of events in the past.

A ▸ Explain to the class that the letter here is a sample answer to the question in 3. Point out that some of the words are missing from the letter, but they don't need to worry about them at this stage.

▸ Ask them to read through the letter, and compare their roleplay dialogue (and visualisation) with the content of the letter in pairs.

Express tip

Read out the advice in this box while students follow in their books. The following exercise provides an opportunity to use time expressions.

B ▸ Have students study the target vocabulary in the box. Teach any vocabulary they do not understand (*eventually = in the end, especially after a lot of delays; over 10 hours = more than 10 hours; on time = at the agreed time; immediately = straightaway, right this moment; delay = extra time due to lateness*). Then ask students to put the words and phrases in the correct places in the letter. Check answers as a class.

ANSWER KEY
1 since; 2 for two weeks; 3 ten days ago; 4 two days; 5 after; 6 eventually; 7 five days later; 8 now; 9 immediately; 10 soon

Support

▸ If necessary, teach the difference between 'for' and 'since': *for* + period of time, but *since* + fixed point in time. Refer students to the two examples in the text and elicit the grammar rule by asking them the question *When do we use 'for' and when do we use 'since'?*

5 Giving reasons for a complaint

Aim: To demonstrate how reported speech can be used to provide support for a letter of complaint.

A ▸ Draw students' attention to the two photographs on the page and explain that the woman is Svetlana and the man is her landlord, Mr. Smith. Have one student read Svetlana's line from the speech bubble. Ask another student in the class what Svetlana said, to elicit *'She told Mr. Smith that her heating system had broken down.'* Write this on the board. Repeat with Mr. Smith's line, and ask another student what he said, eliciting the line quoted in the letter extract in the grey box.

▸ Try to elicit the grammatical differences between direct and reported speech. Reported speech structure is formed by shifting tense in written English, e.g.

from simple present to simple past or from simple past to past perfect. Note that tense shifting is generally considered standard practice in written English but is often omitted in spoken English.

Express tip

Read out the advice in this box while students follow in their books. Point out again to students that visualising the situation before they start writing, including any conversations, will make creating examples to support their arguments easier.

B ‣ Have students reread the letter to find another example of indirect speech. Ask them what they thought were the exact words the speaker used.

ANSWER KEY

Indirect speech: the plumber said he could not fix the problem because the water heater was too old. His exact words were possibly: 'I can't fix the problem because the water heater is too old.'

C ‣ Explain to students that they need to imagine that they are one of Mr. Smith's tenants. Have them read through the list of promises that Mr. Smith made to them when they moved in. Ask them to rewrite those promises as reported speech. If necessary, do the first question as a class.

ANSWER KEY

1 You told us that you were a responsible landlord.
2 You said that you had just installed a new heating and hot water system.
3 You said that we were going to be very happy here.
4 You said that your workmen had always done an excellent job fixing any problems.

6 General Training Writing Task 1: Letter

Aims: To give students the opportunity to consolidate the skills introduced in this unit.

To practise a complete General Training Task 1 Writing task.

To practise writing within a specified time limit.

For this task

‣ Have students read silently through the *For this task* box for a summary of points they need to keep in mind when writing a GT Task 1 letter.
‣ After they have read through the points, ask students to close their books and tell you in their own words what they are. Have students refer back to 2 to review letter openings and closings.

Exam practice

‣ Either set the exam question for homework or do it in class.

Model answer

Dear Mr Phillips,

I am writing this letter to express my deep disappointment with the news that the work placement programme has been cancelled this summer.

One of the main reasons I chose to study Business English at your school in July and August was the chance to participate in the work placement programme. There are many English schools in California that offer Business English, but not many who offer the chance to go and work in a local company as part of the course programme. Your school is more expensive than the competition, but I was happy to pay extra because I thought the course programme was better quality. Now however, I am very unhappy because I have spent a lot of money and I am not getting the course I want.

As the course programme is now very different to the one advertised, I would like to request a full refund of the money I have paid for this course. I will try to contact other schools in California, or maybe New York, which run Business English courses and can guarantee a work placement as part of the course.

I look forward to receiving your reply.

Yours sincerely,

Paisun Seniwong

Writing a General Training Essay

Section aims:
▸ To prepare students for the types of essay questions they can encounter in the exam.
▸ To provide further practice with analysing the exam question, and planning and organising answers.
▸ To teach students how to write an introduction and conclusion for their Task 2 essays.
▸ To introduce and provide practice with Task 2 of the IELTS General Training module.

1 Introduction

Aims: To introduce the type of statements of opinion that students may encounter in the exam.

To give students an opportunity to practise producing arguments in support of a point of view.

A ▸ Draw the class's attention to statement 1 *'Television has a negative influence on children'*. Write it on the board if possible. Ask the class whether they agree or disagree with the statement. Elicit arguments in favour of it, and arguments against it. Write the arguments in two columns on the board.

▸ Have students work alone to read the remaining statements and come up with a list of arguments to support each one. Make sure they know that they are supposed to agree with the statement.

B ▸ Have students discuss their ideas with a partner.

▸ To extend this activity, you could turn it into a pyramid activity. Each pair decides on the best three supporting arguments for each statement. Then the pair joins another pair to compare answers and add or remove ideas, with the aim of coming up with the best three for each argument. Then the group of 4 joins another group to make a group of 8, then the whole class. The class decides on the best arguments as a group, honing suggestions at each stage.

Support

▸ You could come up with one argument for each statement yourself and have the students allocate it to the correct statement, before coming up with their own ideas.

Challenge

▸ If possible, have each pair try to come up with arguments opposing each statement.

In the exam

Draw students' attention to the *In the exam* box. Have them read silently along as you read the information aloud. Remind students that there is a full description of

the GT paper in the *Introduction to the Exam* section at the beginning of the Coursebook.
Ask questions to test students' comprehension.
What kind of topics come up in GT Task 2 questions? What forms might the question take? How many words do candidates need to write? etc.

2 Approaching the question

Aims: To present two essay questions of the type students may encounter in the exam.

To provide practice in analysing the question and deciding on relevant points to include in the answer.

A ▸ Before having students read the question in the book, write *family* and *other important people* on the board. Have students in one half of the class talk about their family with a partner, particularly how important their family is to them. Have the other half of the class discuss in pairs other people in their lives who are important. After a few minutes, have the groups change topics.

▸ Refer students to the exam question in the book and have them underline the keywords. Elicit these from the class.

▸ Remind students that in the exam they need to address the question given, not just something else on that topic. They need to focus on what this specific question requires of them. Have them read the five points and decide which ones they would include in their essay answer.

▸ Check answers as a class.

ANSWER KEY
Points to include are: 2, 3, 4 and 5

Express tip

Read out the advice in this box while students follow in their books. Point out that this A-B-C approach can be used for any writing task.

B ▸ Repeat the procedure above for the new exam question.

C ▸ To lead into the activity, elicit national festivals from the class, and have them tell you what they know about each one. Discuss why festivals are important, e.g. religious, cultural, social purposes, etc.

▸ Write *Guy Fawkes Night* on the board. Elicit from the class anything they know about it. If possible, try to find photographs on the Internet to show the class.

▸ NOTE: Bonfire Night, also known as Guy Fawkes, Guy Fawkes Night or Fireworks Night, is a celebration (but not a public holiday) which takes place on the evening of the 5th November every year in the United Kingdom, New Zealand and formerly Australia, although in recent years, the celebration has spread out to encompass a period of several days or even weeks before or after the exact date. It celebrates the failure of the Gunpowder Plot, in which a group of Catholic conspirators attempted to blow up the British Houses of Parliament along with King James I on that date in 1605.

▸ Explain that the word web is one student's notes in preparation for answering the exam question in 2B. Have students read the notes and answer any vocabulary questions they might have. Point out the system of organisation the student has used for their notes – History, how it is celebrated (what happens during the festival), why it is important. These relate to the keywords in the question.

▸ Have students work alone to create a word web about a festival in their own country. Give them ten minutes to do this. Encourage them to use similar organisation to the example. When they have finished, have them share their outline with a partner.

D ▸ Ask students to read the example plan again and decide if any points are irrelevant to the answer. Elicit suggestions from the class.

Express tip

Read out the advice in this box while students follow in their books. Point out that because in the exam, students will have neither time nor words to include every possible point in their answers, they need to make sure they include only relevant points.

E ▸ Have students read their own plans again and check they have covered all parts of the question and that they haven't included irrelevant material.

3 Organising your essay

Aim: To present a model answer for a Task 2 question, and draw attention to its organisation.

A ▸ Point out to the class that the essay on page 82 is an answer to the question in 2B. Have them read the five paragraph summaries here and match them to the correct paragraph in the essay.

Express tip

Read out the advice in this box while students follow in their books. Point out that Task 2 essays focus on your ability to present and support an argument than on your ability to provide a description of something.

B ▸ Have students compare the essay to the original question and, in pairs, decide if the student answered the actual task.

4 Introducing and concluding your essay

Aim: To introduce and practise techniques for writing essay introductions and conclusions.

▸ Draw the class's attention to the exam question. Put students in groups of three. One student in each group reads introduction 1, one reads introduction 2 and one reads introduction 3. Each student must decide whether the introduction they have read is a good introduction to an essay answering the question, and why or why not. They must share their ideas with other two members of the group. Have each group decide together on the best introduction. Elicit answers from the class.

Express tip

Read out the advice in this box while students follow in their books. Point out that their introduction may paraphrase the statement in the question in their own words, but they will lose marks for just copying down the question as it is.

B ▸ Follow the same procedure as the preceding step, dividing the class again into the same groups of three.

ANSWER KEY

Conclusion 2 is the most effective. Conclusion 1 doesn't relate to the question. Conclusion 3 is far too short and doesn't recap any of the arguments made in the essay.

C ▸ Have students read the conclusions again to underline the opening phrases. Point out that they should memorise these phrases and use them to begin the conclusions in their own essays.

ANSWER KEY

1 To sum up; 2 In conclusion; 3 In summary

Express tip

Read out the advice in this box while students follow in their books. Point out that that conclusion 2 in 4B does this effectively, while conclusions 1 and 3 do not do this.

D ▸ Have students decide on a festival in their own country and write the opening and conclusion for an essay answering the question in 2B. To place them under time pressure, give them no more than half an hour for this task. When they have finished, have them share their work with a partner.
▸ You could 'publish' them on the walls for students to vote on which one they think is best.

---

5 General Training Writing Task 2: Essay

Aims: To give students the opportunity to consolidate the skills introduced in this unit.

To practise a complete General Training Task 2 Writing task.

To practise writing within a specified time limit.

For this task

▸ Have students read silently through the *For this task* box for a summary of points they need to keep in mind when writing a GT Task 2 letter.
▸ After reading through the points, ask students to close their books and tell you in their own words what they are.

Exam practice

▸ Either set the exam question for homework or have students do it in class.

Support

▸ Analyse the question together as a class and decide what it is asking and not asking. Together as a class, or in groups, have students create a plan for an answer, and then write it from plan in 20–30 minutes.

Model answer

In certain cultures, such as many Asian or Middle Eastern ones, it is common to live in extended families. In these families, weaker or more vulnerable people are protected and taken care of. This sense of responsibility towards other family members is not always shared in all contemporary societies. Yet I believe we have an obligation to try to look after this section of the community.

In my opinion, our society has to provide ways of ensuring that the people who really need help receive it. We cannot always rely on families to give this support, for a variety of reasons. For example, some people don't have time or enough money to look after other family members. In cases such as this, somebody has to help. This is why we need national organisations such as the Salvation Army to look after the vulnerable members of society. These types of groups are private; therefore, they need proper funding.

Individuals such as you or I can give donations to help them. What's more, some organisations accept help in other forms: donations of food, clothing or blankets. It is even possible to volunteer your time, by helping at the weekend or in the evening.

Furthermore, the government should use part of the income it receives from our taxes to build and run centres which can cater for the old or the handicapped. Our taxes should be used to benefit our society in this way in addition to helping the country run efficiently for things like the police and ambulances. By doing this, the government can adopt a nationwide approach and employ suitably qualified staff.

In brief, I strongly believe that it is essential that we take care of the weaker members of society through governmental and private organisations such as the Salvation Army.

The Practice test

The *IELTS Express Coursebook* contains a complete practice test for the IELTS exam. This test is a true reflection of the different levels of questions and tasks in the IELTS exam.

It is recommended that you use this test as a mock examination after students have completed the Coursebook, shortly before they take the actual exam. Answer keys, including model writing answers, and listening scripts are provided in this Teacher's Guide.

How to administer the Practice test

Ideally, in order to give your students as accurate a simulation of the IELTS exam as possible, you should give all of the sections back-to-back in a single day, although sometimes the Speaking exam may be taken on a different day. However, this will require at least $2\frac{3}{4}$ hours for the Listening, Reading and Writing papers, not including short breaks between papers. You may prefer to do it a paper at a time, over a few days.

Remember that no dictionaries or any other reference books may be used in any part of the IELTS exam.

Before the test, enlarge and photocopy enough copies of the two answer sheets on page 128 of the Coursebook for every student. You will also need blank writing paper for students to use for the Writing section. Insist that there is no talking throughout the exam and make sure everyone's mobile phone is turned off before the exam.

IELTS Part 1: Listening

Time: up to 30 minutes, plus 10 minutes to transfer answers.

External noise, traffic, etc can be very distracting during a listening exam so try to find a quiet room or a quiet time of day to conduct this section. Students who arrive late will be very distracting to the rest of the class, so strongly encourage students to arrive on time.

You can play the tape or CD on a player positioned at the front of the room, but make sure it is loud enough for everyone to hear. Alternatively, you could use a language lab, but remind students that in the actual test a cassette player will be used.

▸ Distribute answer sheets to the class and have students write their names at the top of the sheet. Tell students that during the listening they are to record their answers in their Coursebook and that at the end of the exam they will be given ten minutes to transfer their answers to this special answer sheet.

▸ Have students open their books to page 84. Play the recording ONCE ONLY. Do not stop or pause the recording, but just let it play through to the end.

▸ When the recording has finished, inform students that they now have ten minutes to transfer their answers to the answer sheet, using a PENCIL. Tell them they must be very careful to record their answer in the appropriate place – candidates often lose marks for not doing this. Remind them that correct spelling is important and also that they must observe any word limits for particular questions. After five and nine minutes, announce how long they have left.

▸ After ten minutes, collect answer sheets for marking.

IELTS Part 2: Reading

Time: 1 hour

▸ Distribute answer sheets to the class and have students write their names at the top of the sheet. Tell students that they are to record their answers on the answer sheet IN PENCIL as they do the exam. Unlike the Listening exam, there is no extra time given for this.

▸ Ask your students to open their Coursebooks at the appropriate page. Remember that there is a General Training option (page 100) or an Academic Training option (page 88). Make sure they do the right one! Explain that students have only one hour to read all three texts. Write the start time and finish time on a board at the front of the room, but remind them that the questions can be done in any order.

▸ Announce when there are only five minutes remaining. When one hour is up, insist that they finish immediately, then collect answer sheets for marking.

IELTS Part 3: Writing

Time: 1 hour

▸ Make sure that students have enough writing paper, and have some spare sheets at the front. Have students write their names at the top of each piece of paper they use. Have students use a different sheet of paper for Tasks 1 and 2 – this reflects exam procedure.

▸ Ask your students to open their Coursebooks at the appropriate page. Remember that there is a General Training option (page 108) or an Academic Training option (page 97). Make sure they do the right one! Explain that students have only one hour to answer both questions. Write the start time and finish time on a board at the front of the room. Remind them that they should spend approximately 20 minutes on Part 1 and 40 minutes on Part 2. Tell them they can answer the questions in any order.

▸ Announce when there are only five minutes remaining. When one hour is up, insist that they finish immediately, then collect answer sheets for marking.

IELTS Part 4: Speaking

Time: Following the procedure below, approximately 1 hour.
Each interview typically lasts between 12 and 15 minutes. This means that even with a relatively small class, conducting the practice test individually would take several hours. You may choose to do this, but the procedure outlined below will enable you to save a great deal of time.
Note: If you have the *IELTS Express Speaking Video/DVD,* you should show it to your class before conducting this test to help them understand what they should be focusing on in the exam.

▸ Make a photocopy of the topic card for Part 2 of the Speaking exam from page 99 of the Coursebook.

▸ Remind the class of the examiner's criteria for the Speaking exam, by writing these terms on the board:
Fluency and coherence; Lexical resource; Grammatical range and accuracy; Pronunciation
These criteria are explained in the section 'What are the Examiners looking for?' in the introduction on page 4 of this book, and also in the *IELTS Express Speaking Video/DVD*.

▸ Divide the class into four groups, and allocate one criterion to each group. As you interview the model candidate, ask the class to listen carefully, and evaluate the candidate on their criterion, taking notes on *Good points* and *Areas for improvement*.

▸ Persuade a reasonably strong and confident member of the class to 'volunteer' to do the exam in front of the class. Tell them that you will play the examiner and they are to imagine that they do not know you and you do not know them. Using the questions and question cards on page 99, you will conduct a mock Speaking exam with a student to provide a model for the rest of the class.

▸ When the Speaking exam finishes, praise the candidate for doing it in front of their classmates. Ask the class for positive comments on each of the examiners' criteria and then areas in which the candidate could improve.

▸ Now divide the class into pairs or groups of three. The pairs will take it in turns to play examiner and candidate, using the same material from page 99 as the candidate. In the groups of three, one student could act as an observer. Each interview should last at least 10 minutes. Encourage them to give feedback on each other's performance. If you are concerned that students may become familiar with the material if they all use the same questions, you can photocopy the Speaking Topic cards on page 115 of this book and give one pile to each group. 'Examiners' can then draw one card from this pile at random for the test.

▸ While the interviews are underway, circulate and monitor taking notes – making sure that you, and students acting as examiners, are evaluating and giving feedback based on the IELTS criteria. When all groups have finished, invite some of them to comment on each other's performances, and feed in your comments as appropriate.

Marking and Grading the Papers

Listening and Reading

Use the answer key provided in the *Teacher's Guide* to mark the answer sheets. Answers are considered either right or wrong. There are no half marks awarded. Answers with spelling mistakes are considered as incorrect.

The way in which a candidate's marks on the IELTS exam are converted into an IELTS band score is confidential and varies slightly from one test paper to another. However, an approximate guide to what candidates may achieve can be determined according to the following table.

Note: This chart is very approximate, and should serve as a guide only. It is by no means definitive.

Band	Listening score	Academic Training Reading score	General Training Reading score
4	9	8	15
5	16	15	23
6	23	23	30
7	30	30	34
8	35	35	37

Writing and Speaking

Grading candidates' performance in these two areas is much more complicated and examiners undergo extensive training to learn how to do this. The examiners criteria for Writing and Speaking on page 4, should assist you in evaluating your students' work. Model writing answers are provided on page 96–97.

For further information visit www.ielts.org

Listening

Section 1

1 telephone; **2** 14 King Street; **3** AP12 7QT; **4** hairdryer;
5 10; **6** garden; **7** Wednesday; **8** C; **9** G; **10** B

Section 2

11 C; **12** A; **13** C; **14** A; **15** C; **16** A; **17** gentle exercise
18 weight lifting; **19** healthy living; **20** relaxation

Section 3

21 cold weather; **22** young mothers; **23** statistics seminar
24 C; **25** D; **26** (the) main square; **27** age groups
28 (a) cookery competition; **29** (the) town hall
30 head of education

Section 4

31 B; **32** A; **33** A; **34** C; **35** smart cards; **36** computers
37 comfortable; **38** detailed information; **39** suburban
40 environmental issues

Academic Reading

Reading passage 1

1 shadoof; **2** crops; domestic purposes (in either order)
3 (large) (pottery) jars; **4** sanitation; **5** (the) arch
6 lead pipes; **7** F; **8** B; **9** A; **10** C; **11** (a) mirror
12 (the) shop's door; **13** hydraulics

Reading passage 2

14 vi; **15** iii **16** ix; **17** ii; **18** x; **19** v
20 reintroduction programme
21 recreationalists
22 (the) colonization front
23 lethal control
24, 25, 26 A, D, E (in any order)

Reading passage 3

27 privacy; **28** asthenia; **29** isolation; sensory deprivation
(in either order); **30** D; **31** A; **32** D; **33** C; **34** A; **35** B
36 familiarity; **37** amazement; **38** cooperation; **39** tension
40 violence

Academic Writing

Sample answers

Writing Task 1

The two types of goods that people spent the greatest amount of money on were electrical goods and groceries. Men spent far more than women on electrical goods and women spent far more than men on groceries.

The next highest spending was on clothing and footwear and in this category women had a considerably higher share of the market than men. Women also spent a lot more than men on furniture and floor coverings and health and beauty products, although expenditure on these was much lower in comparison with some of the other types of goods. Women also had a higher share of the market for homewares and books. Men, on the other hand, spent a great deal more than women on DIY goods and music and video.

However, although women had a higher share of the market than men in the majority of categories listed in the table, men and women were about equal in terms of the actual sums of money spent. In fact, men spent slightly more than women.

Writing Task 2

It is certainly true that the situation regarding careers has changed a lot in recent times. In the past, it was quite common for people to stay in the same job from the time they left school until the time they retired, but that has become quite rare these days.

One reason is that the world of work has changed enormously. The arrival of the computer and information technology has meant that a lot of jobs that people had in the past have ceased to exist. As a result, people have had to get new skills and move into different types of work. And changes in the way work is done keep on happening, so it is not possible for people to remain in the same jobs forever – they have to adapt to developments and get new skills.

Another reason is that there are no longer many jobs that are completely secure. In the business world, companies buy other companies, companies go out of business and companies change the nature of what they do, and all these things can result in people losing their jobs or changing their jobs.

In addition, attitudes have changed and it is no longer considered strange for people to move from one job to another. In the past, it was assumed that people would stay in the same job but now the attitude is that people should have a variety of experience.

In my view, this is a good thing. It can be dull to do the same thing for years and years and work is much more interesting if you change your job from time to time. Also, it can be hard to decide on what you want to do when you are very young. These days, you can change your mind and move into a completely different kind of work if you want to. This makes it more possible than it was in the past for people to have jobs that they find interesting.

General Training Reading

Section 1

1 F; 2 D; 3 H; 4 B; 5 J; 6 G; 7 A; 8 tennis shots
9 action replay; 10 inventions; 11 throwing abilities
12 trainers; 13 fitness; 14 (branded) souvenirs

Section 2

15 (the) Youth Worker; 16 The Refectory; 17 The Restaurant
18 (the/a) security team; 19 respected
20 (its/the) enrolments; 21 TRUE; 22 NOT GIVEN; 23 TRUE
24 NOT GIVEN; 25 FALSE; 26 FALSE; 27 FALSE

Section 3

28 box of matches; 29 (a/an) (brief) outline; 30 (a) full replica; 31 (some) rule changes; 32 Tadpole Games
33 Selective Laser Sintering; 34 rubber trees 35 H; 36 C
37 J; 38 I; 39 B; 40 A

General Training Writing

Sample answers
Writing Task 1

Dear Sir/Madam,

I am an international student in my second year of the Business Administration course at the college. My tutor is Mr Patterson, and I am a full-time student, living in the college residence.

I am writing to request a week's leave from the college next month. The wedding of a member of my family is taking place in my home country then and it is very important that I attend this. One of my cousins is getting married, and my family expect me to be there. Although this will mean that I

have to miss lectures for a week, I can arrange for one of my friends on the course to give me any notes concerning what I have missed.

I would be grateful if you would give me permission to be absent for the week beginning 15th April. If you are kind enough to allow me to do this, I will speak to Mr Patterson and arrange to make up for any work that I did not do while I was away.

Yours faithfully,

Writing Task 2

I think it is certainly true that some people take too much interest in the lives of celebrities. A lot of so-called 'celebrities' are not very interesting people anyway. Often they are not very talented and they are given far more attention and publicity than they deserve.

Some people become obsessed with certain celebrities. They read about them in all sorts of magazines and some even try to copy them, particularly in the way they look. In some cases this can lead to serious problems, such as eating disorders that can result when girls want to be as thin as a celebrity they particularly admire.

Another problem is that some celebrities are not good examples for young people. They behave badly in their private lives and this bad behaviour gets a lot of publicity. This could have a bad influence on young people who admire these celebrities and may think it is cool to copy them.

Some people say that taking a big interest in celebrities and what they do is harmless, and that it gives some people entertainment that takes their minds off their own boring or difficult lives. I suppose this is true to a certain extent, but I think it could also be said that the amount of interest in celebrities is a bad sign. It shows that in the modern world many people care too much about something that is rather silly, instead of paying attention to the important things in life. I think it is wrong for people to fill their minds with rubbish about people who will be completely forgotten in a very short time when there are serious things they should be giving their attention to.

Listening script

Section 1

Judith: Hello.

Hilary: Hello. This is Hilary. I'm calling about the house. I'm moving in next week.

Judith: Oh, yes, Hilary. This is Judith. I met you when you came to look at the house.

Hilary: Yes. I just had a few more questions I wanted to ask.

Judith: Of course.

Hilary: Well, first, about the rent. I realise I didn't check what it included.

Judith: Yes, that's important! It includes most things. We don't have to pay extra for heating, for example, just for the telephone, which is fair enough, I suppose. Local taxes are part of the rent, so that's not a worry.

Hilary: That's fine. Then, I remember I should have sent my letter of reference to the landlord by now. But I haven't got his address.

Judith: Yes, you should get that off right away. Address it to Mr Crawley. He's at <u>14 King Street</u> …

Hilary: Is that in Exford?

Judith: Yes. And then you'll need to put the post code, of course. It's AP12 …

Hilary: Uh-huh.

Judith: <u>7QT</u>.

Hilary: Got that. Thanks.

Judith: I also realise I don't know exactly what the house has, in the way of equipment. Is there a microwave, for example?

Hilary: There isn't. None of us feels the need.

Judith: Oh fine. I'm sure I can do without one, too. What about a <u>hairdryer</u>?

Hilary: Maybe you should bring one if you need one.

Judith: <u>I'll buy one</u>, yes. And TV?

Hilary: Oh, yes, we've got two, in fact.

Judith: Was there anything else?

Hilary: I just wondered if there were any rules?

Judith: Not really. We share the cleaning, things like that. We do have to be careful about loud music.

Hilary: Yes.

Judith: So we've agreed that there shouldn't be any loud music after 9, and that we don't play music at all in the living room after <u>10</u>. Up to 11 in your own room's OK, as long as it's not too noisy.

Hilary: That's sounds good. And is there somewhere safe I can keep my bike?

Judith: That's difficult. To be honest, lots do get stolen round here. We haven't got a garage, so we tend to park ours in the <u>garden</u>, so that they're hidden from the street.

Hilary: OK.

Judith: Now, I hope you like cooking.

Hilary: Yes, I do. Do you all have shared meals?

Judith: Not very often, actually. But when the weather's good in the summer, we like to have a barbecue together, which we do each <u>Wednesday</u>. We tend to go out at weekends.

Hilary: Sounds fun!

Judith: Are you familiar with this area?

Hilary: A bit. Actually, there a few things that I'd like to know the location of. A bank, for example.

Judith: Yes, there's one quite close. You just <u>go up to the junction near the house, the one where four roads meet, and go straight ahead, and then take the second left. It's a little way down there, on the left-hand side.</u>

Hilary: That's convenient. Another thing, is that I like to check my emails quite often. I was wondering how far away an Internet café was?

Judith: Well, there are a couple, actually, but one's much cheaper than the other. The one I use is very handy. You just <u>go up to the big junction and then, well, I go straight ahead and then turn right, so that it's on the right-hand side.</u>

Hilary: Fine. And one last thing.

Judith: Uh-huh.

Hilary: I need to go to the post office quite often. I'm hoping there's one quite close to the house.

Judith: You're in luck. You'd walk <u>up to the big junction, and then, if you want a nice route, take the street that's slightly to the right. Then you'd want the second left, and you'd find it on the right side of the street.</u>

Hilary: Well, it all sounds great.

Judith: So, we'll see you in a couple of days' time?

Hilary: Yes. OK, bye.

Judith: Bye.

Section 2

Man: Next, I'd like to welcome Carol Browne, manager of the Apollo Leisure Centre. Carol, welcome.

Woman: Thank you.

Man: Now, Carol, the Apollo seems a familiar sight, but how long has it actually been here?

Woman: Well, we started negotiations to take over the previous Active Life Centre, that used to occupy the premises, in 2000, and planned to open in 2001, although the usual delays meant <u>it was 2002 before we were up and running</u>.

Man: And do you have quite a mix of members, or are you focused on certain groups?

Woman: It's pretty broad, actually. <u>There are something like 200 adult members, so that's our biggest group, but we also have as many as 100 youth members, together with about 50 family group members</u> – and I think we'll see that section growing to 100 over the next couple of years.

Man: Healthy numbers!

Woman: Yes, and we'll be developing the Centre, to make it yet more attractive. We're hoping eventually to build in a rock climbing wall, which would make a useful addition. We've already opened our swimming pool, which is hugely popular, and <u>we'll have a massage room open within twelve months</u>.

Man: Now, I understand you have different categories of membership?

Woman: Yes, to suit every pocket. Blue membership includes all facilities for the member and a guest at all times, which is good for people with unpredictable timetables. If you can make it during daytime hours, <u>red membership gives you excellent returns for your fee, as for only half price you can use all the facilities during the day – and they're actually less crowded then</u>. Green membership is designed for people who are only able to come infrequently, and so of course costs less.

Man: And there are chances to socialise?

Woman: Oh, certainly. Our café is very popular, and is a nice place to wind down and chat after working out or whatever. In fact, <u>while it used to shut at 8, we've extended that to 9 now, with last orders taken at 8.30</u>. It serves a whole range of food and drink.

Man: So, if someone wants to join, what do they do?

Woman: Come and see us! We'll give you all the details. The induction process takes about an hour and a quarter, which includes <u>three quarters of an hour, on average, with a personal trainer</u>, and something like half an hour being shown round the different facilities.

Man: So we'd be well looked after.

Woman: Definitely.

Man: OK, now, Carol, can you give us some idea of what we could expect to get as members of Apollo?

Woman: Sure. Well, let's take next Monday as an example. The early evening would begin with the programme of classes. Of course, members would also be at liberty to do their own thing. I'm just talking about the listed classes that we'll be offering.

Man: Uh-huh.

Woman: So, let's say you're free to turn up at 4pm. You could spend an hour in a class that we call <u>Gentle Exercise</u>. This isn't a hard work-out as you might be imagining it, but a session designed for those who perhaps are not used to rigorous classes and would like something to ease them in.

Man: Right.

Woman: The next thing on offer will be starting at 5, and again it'll last for an hour. In contrast, this is what we simply call <u>Weight Lifting</u>. It's certainly not for softies, but this strenuous session is of course carefully monitored, and we wouldn't let anyone do anything silly.

Man: Well, that's reassuring.

Woman: And then, kicking off at quarter past six, you'll be welcome at a class aimed at promoting better life styles, which we run under the banner of <u>Healthy Living</u>. We'll give you all sorts of useful advice about just living better ...

Man: Sounds easier than working out ...

Woman: And probably at least as important!

Man: And rounds the evening off nicely.

Woman: Oh no, we still have one more offering. These days, so many people are working, frankly, more than they should be, and we try to combat the stress that that creates by encouraging those who can to take part in the class we call <u>Relaxation</u>. You can learn lots of helpful techniques for staying calm when you think everything's going terribly.

Man: Now you're talking!

Woman: So we'll see you on Monday?

Man: Ah, now ...

Section 3

Dr Hurst: So, Aldo, how's it going so far with your assignment?

Aldo: Not too bad.

Dr Hurst: You're looking at the community round here?

Aldo: That's right – how people perceive the community they are in.

Dr Hurst: Have you made much progress?

Aldo: Hmm. I conducted quite a lot of interviews on the street with local residents. The responses are interesting. I haven't got quite as many, yet, as I'd like. I had wondered if I'd have language problems, particularly with the different accents. I seem to have managed, though. Having to work in the open has made it harder, and with the cold weather there's been recently, people don't necessarily want to stop and talk, like they do if it's nice and sunny – that's something I've had to deal with. Of course, some people are too busy to stop and talk, but that's OK.

Dr Hurst: I see. So have you formed a good overall picture of how people view the community?

Aldo: To an extent. I've certainly talked to plenty of older people – I guess they may have more time to talk. I still don't really have enough young mothers, though – I've managed to get enough older mothers and children through the schools ... that's something I had been worried about.

Dr Hurst: Well, that shouldn't be too hard. Now, how are you going to deal with all the data you've collected?

Aldo: That's the difficult part! I guess I need to run some analyses, but I'm rather unclear about what methods to use ...

Dr Hurst: You've told me you're confident about using computers, so you just need some input on choosing programmes. You should attend a statistics seminar. They're held every Friday, after the methodology seminars, in Room 105. That should help you to select an approach.

Aldo: Oh, good, I'll do that.

Dr Hurst: Meanwhile, let's hear something about what you've learnt.

Aldo: Yes. I talked to a number of residents.

Dr Hurst: Good. I imagine they didn't always have the same opinions!

Aldo: Views were certainly quite mixed. Take sports facilities – in general people seemed to think they weren't very good ... there's no swimming pool in the area, for example ... but at the same time there's new football training area – it looks very smart to me, but it doesn't seem to get used very much. People seem to prefer sitting around in the parks. They enjoy that, taking picnics and so on – although they want the council to be more efficient at cleaning ... there's a lot of litter. People are obviously very concerned about their children's learning. The general view seems to be that early schooling, at primary level, is of a good standard in the area, but that this standard declines as children move up through the system ... the colleges were criticised in particular.

Dr Hurst: OK. Now, are you going to collect any more data?

Aldo: Some, I hope. There's a local festival next week, and I think the events there will give me some useful opportunities. I talked to a council officer about it all.

Dr Hurst: Good. What does it involve?

Aldo: First, there's a dance show, which I'm sure I'll enjoy. The council explained that the concert hall's being renovated, and won't be ready in time, so it's being held in the Main Square, which I think will be better anyway – at least I'll have more space to wander round in.

Dr Hurst: True.

Aldo: And so I hope to be able to carefully watch the age groups that are there in the audience, and make notes about how they interact. So that's one event. Then, the following day, there's another interesting event which I look forward to going along to, and that's a cookery competition.

Dr Hurst: Oh yes? Interesting.

Aldo: I think so. Yes, that one's being organised in the Town Hall, which has a big space, apparently. With food and cooking from all the different people in the area, the council officer told me that it'll be a good chance to find out about the different cultures that comprise the community.

Dr Hurst: Sounds promising.

Aldo: Then there's one more event I'd like to go along to. The council officer promised me that the courses fair will be interesting. It's going to be in the Langtree Theatre, and the officer said lots of teachers will be there. I've already talked to plenty of them, but he advised me to try and ask some questions with the Head of Education, who will be there.

Dr Hurst: That's all very useful. OK, I suggest you come back next ...

Section 4

That big cities around the world are getting bigger is a clear trend. This situation is going to make the issue of transport increasingly important. Cities cannot work if their people, and their visitors, cannot move around. This means that public transport is vital to the success of cities. And yet private car ownership is increasing all the time. Can these two facts be contained in the same reality? Isn't the car slowly, but surely, strangling the city? But we must acknowledge it does have genuine benefits. Having said that, the fact that car owners can escape to the mountains is of little relevance to the issue of daily city life, in which we need to do things like ferry heavy shopping and luggage around – something the car of course is invaluable for. But the so-called family car is rarely occupied by a family, just a single driver taking up a lot of road space. It's not only the car that clogs up our roads, of course. Trucks are heavy, noisy and smelly intruders. But it's hard to persuade companies to opt for rail freight in favour of road. They argue that it is cheaper and more flexible, and <u>trucks are undoubtedly able to go when you want where you want</u>. The cost claim is false, however – truck companies don't hold themselves responsible for the environmental costs they incur, nor are they keen to calculate the time spent on repairs or delays. So, this is our first challenge – the sheer volume of traffic. If we compare three developed and urbanised countries, we can see interesting differences. The UK, for example, has just over 20 million cars – 1 per every 3 people, approximately – and nearly 3 million buses and trucks. These figures sound very high, but in fact, the Netherlands, although only a little over a quarter the population, has more vehicles per head of population. Meanwhile <u>Germany, bigger than both other countries put together, actually outstrips either in terms of vehicles per head of population</u>. Now, there is no correlation between these figures and the percentages of journeys made on public transport. This means that the route to better public transport use is not abolishing the car, but rather making public transport better. Not surprisingly, where people can choose, they choose the thing they prefer, not the thing they don't. How do people judge public transport? Well, a major survey was carried out this year, indicating that there are many aspects, from clean interiors of buses to the proximity of routes to homes and workplaces. Fare prices is a complex issue, and needs to be accounted with car costs. <u>What people seemed to find most frustrating is scheduling. If the route doesn't pass their departure point when it suits them, they'll drive instead</u>. The issue of personal safety seems to have reduced in urgency, with better lighting at stops and CCTV.

Now, various measures are being taken in a number of major cities, all designed to increase the appeal of public transport, and thus to persuade car users to leave their cars behind, and free up the city's roads. Among these is bringing in <u>smart cards</u> – these are purchased in advance and mean passengers spend less time waiting to buy tickets and board buses and trains, particularly when switching across transport modes within the same journey. Another initiative is the use of <u>computers</u> in managing scheduling with greater efficiency. But such logistical measures are not sufficient in themselves – and indeed the benefits that they bring are often less apparent to passengers than to transport managers. From the passengers' point of view, the fact that buses are becoming more <u>comfortable</u> is significant, because it brings them more in line with the car. Delays and diversions are of course deeply irritating for passengers. Even if these can't be eliminated, ensuring that passengers have more <u>detailed information</u> available to them will help to reduce their sense of stress. We often associate public transport with inner-city travel, but of direct benefit to passengers, are systems such as taxi-sharing and dial-a-bus which provide more flexible options for <u>suburban</u> journeys. And finally, nothing really significant can happen without a shift in people's mind-sets. The way we travel is an expression of our values about many things. Companies operating public transport are slowly, but

surely, finding it possible to sell their services as a public-spirited alternative to the car, as awareness of <u>environmental issues</u> has increased radically in the last few years. Overall, then, this combination of steps and changes has a good chance of shifting the city out of the car and onto the bus and train.

Speaking

Part 1

Examiner:	Let's talk about where you live. What kind of place is it?
Candidate:	I live in the UK, in Cambridge. It's most famous for the university. It's quite a small town with lots of old buildings and green spaces.
Examiner:	What do you like best about Cambridge?
Candidate:	It's very peaceful and you can walk everywhere easily.
Examiner:	What kinds of jobs do people do in Cambridge?
Candidate:	A lot of people work for the university of course and there are many new computer companies as well.
Examiner:	And would you say Cambridge is a good place to work in?
Candidate:	Yes, it is because there are plenty of opportunities.
Examiner:	Now let's move on to sport. How much time do you spend playing or watching sports?
Candidate:	Not very much – maybe a couple of hours a week.
Examiner:	Which sports are most popular in the UK?
Candidate:	Football, rugby and golf. Actually, I've read that fishing is the most popular hobby in the UK. I'm not sure if that's a sport!
Examiner:	Which sports did you do when you were at school?
Candidate:	I did hockey and netball in the winter and athletics and tennis in the summer.
Examiner:	Do you think all children should do some sport?
Candidate:	Yes, I think it's a good idea for children to learn to do some different physical activities. Through sport, they can learn about teamwork and achieving something through effort and skill.
Examiner:	Now let's move on to food. Do you like cooking?
Candidate:	No, not much – but I do like food!
Examiner:	How often do you go to restaurants?
Candidate:	Quite often – about twice a week on average.
Examiner:	What kinds of restaurants do you enjoy eating in?

Candidate: I like restaurants that aren't too formal. I prefer the cosy kind! But it's very important to me that the food is fresh and healthy.

Examiner: What does a restaurant need to do to be successful?

Candidate: I think a good restaurant should change its menu fairly frequently and use food that is in season at a particular time of year. It needs to consider the kinds of customers it's trying to attract and give them good service.

Part 2

Examiner: I'd like you to describe a shop that you enjoy going to.

Candidate: I'm going to talk about a shop in Cambridge that I like going to. It's in the centre of Cambridge and about five minutes' walk from my house. It's called the Coffee Shop, and as you can imagine it sells coffee! It has a big range of coffee beans from different countries and you can choose which ones you want and the lady will grind them up for you. The smell is delicious – and the coffee is too. The shop also sells lots of different teas and teapots, coffee pots, cups and saucers as well as other nice things for your kitchen. They also sell a few very expensive chocolates. I tend to go there about once a week – normally on Saturday and I buy enough coffee to last for the next week. I enjoy going there not just because of the nice coffee, but also because the lady who works there is very friendly. I often help her with her crossword! So, that's my favourite shop.

Examiner: Do your friends like this shop too?

Candidate: Yes, they do. It's a very popular place.

Part 3

Examiner: We've been talking about a shop that enjoy going to and I'd like to discuss with you one or two more general questions related to this. Let's consider first of all developments in shopping. Are there certain kinds of shops that are becoming more popular?

Candidate: Well I suppose shops that sell computers and computer games and also those that sell mobile phones. There seem to be more and more of them opening up. I suppose it's not surprising, but I find these shops rather boring personally!

Examiner: What disadvantages do you think there may be to an increase in consumerism?

Candidate: For me, one of the main disadvantages is that increased consumerism seems to emphasise the

difference between rich and poor people. Also another disadvantage is many people already work too hard and with the increase in consumerism they drive themselves harder and harder just to make money to buy things they don't actually need or have time to enjoy!

Examiner: In what ways do you think advertising affects people's attitudes?

Candidate: The more advertising there is, the more people seem to want and they're never satisfied with what they've got. I suppose it really depends what you mean by advertising. Some of it could be seen as socially useful – for example advertising campaigns about healthy eating.

Examiner: In what ways do you think shopping may change in the future?

Candidate: Well, I'm sure there will be an increase in online shopping because more and more people have access to home computers. I also think that many small shops in the centre of towns will close down and bigger and bigger supermarkets will open on the outskirts. In some ways it may be more convenient, but I don't know if these changes will really improve our lives.

The Speaking Video/DVD

About the Speaking Video

There is a speaking video or DVD available for both *IELTS Express Intermediate* and *IELTS Express Upper intermediate*. Each video/ DVD is approximately 38 minutes long and features a complete candidate interview conducted by a qualified IELTS examiner. This section contains photocopiable activities for your students to do while they watch the video, and a transcript for the video.

The Video consists of five parts:

1, an overview unit, in which the examiner explains in detail the criteria by which a candidate's performance is assessed;
2, 3 and **4,** a description of each of the three parts of the IELTS Speaking exam, giving tips on performance appropriate to each section, e.g.
- Part 1: The examiner talks about extending responses and using 'fillers' such as 'sort of', 'you know' and 'anyway.'
- Part 2: The examiner talks about writing notes before beginning the long turn and how to clarify questions.
- Part 3: The examiner talks about demonstrating a wide vocabulary and using conditional sentences.

5, a complete model interview: an uninterrupted recording of a full three-part Speaking exam taken by a candidate at the appropriate level.

Throughout, points are illustrated using clips of 'model candidates' of different nationalities performing a simulated IELTS Speaking exam. Some are examples of good language usage, some are not so good, but these 'model candidates' have all been specially selected to reflect the grade of each Coursebook and so provide a realistic level for students to aim for.

Using the Speaking Video/DVD in your class

The *Speaking Video* reflects and builds on what students have learned about the Speaking exam in the Speaking sections of the Coursebook. Although you could choose to show the video in instalments, after students have been introduced to the relevant section in the Speaking sections of their Coursebook, the video can also be used as a revision aid a few days before students attempt the Practice test. This would really help students to consolidate what they have learned throughout the course, but it is also useful because the Practice test uses similar – but not the same – material to the examinations on the *Speaking Video*.

Ideally, if you have time, it would be advantageous to show the video twice. Once before the students take the Coursebook practice test and once after, providing a good opportunity for reflection on what candidates need to demonstrate in order to achieve the grade they want at IELTS.

The accompanying photocopiable activities for each section should be given to students before they watch the video, for them to fill in as they watch. Answers are provided in the answer key. If necessary, the video transcript here can also be photocopied and given to your students.

IELTS Speaking Module Overview
(I = Interviewer; E = Examiner)

I: We're here today to talk about the Speaking module of the IELTS Exam, and which skills and techniques students need to develop to be successful.
We asked an experienced IELTS Examiner and teacher, Ranald Barnicot, of Barnet College in North London, first to examine eight candidates at different levels from different nationalities, then to analyse their performances in each part of the Speaking module, and finally to assemble a range of extracts to illustrate these skills and techniques.

I: Tell me about the IELTS Speaking module.

E: Well, there are three parts in all, lasting between 11 and 14 minutes. The interview is one-to-one, thus candidates are examined individually, not in pairs.

I: Before you tell me what happens in each Part, what is the examiner looking for in general?

E: Well, there are four criteria with which we assess candidates. They are: Fluency and coherence; Vocabulary; Accuracy and range of grammar; and Pronunciation.

I: 'Fluency' means being able to speak naturally and without too much hesitation, right?

E: Yes, and not pausing to correct yourself too much. Also, speaking at a proper speed, not too slow and not too fast. 'Coherence' means that your speech is structured, it's well organised.

I: I understand 'vocabulary' and 'pronunciation'. Accurate grammar is correct grammar, clearly, but what about 'range' of grammar?

E: Basically, it means being able to use a wide selection of grammatical forms and sentence structures.

I: So not too simple?

E: Precisely.

IELTS Speaking Module Part 1

I: What happens in the first part of the exam?

E: In this part, candidates have to answer a number of questions about themselves – their likes and dislikes, habits, plans, etc, and also maybe about people in their country. The subjects might be: sport, travel, food, family life and so on.

I: Is there anything candidates should concentrate on when answering these questions?

E: Yes, one important thing is giving extended responses.

I: You mean, long answers?

E: Yes, not just one word answers or even just a short, simple phrase or sentence. Let's look at this candidate, Cat.

E: Morning.

Cat: Morning.

E: My name is Ranald Barnicot. Can you tell me your full name?

Cat: OK. My name is Bai Ru Jiang but you can call me Cat.

E: OK, Cat. Tell me, please, where do you come from?

Cat: I come from China – from the north – sorry, south of China – it's near the sea – it's a very beautiful city – it's called Nan ning.

I: Yes, she gave a lot of extra information, didn't she? And she obviously wanted to communicate.

E: Yes, now look at Gina and Ahmad.

Ahmad: My full name is Ahmad Mohseni.

E: Uh-huh. And where do you come from Ahmad?

Ahmad: I come from the Netherlands.

E: Which sport is the most popular in your country?

Gina: Football.

E: Ahmad used rather short sentences. I mean, where did he come from in the Netherlands, and what else is there to say about it? And Gina just answered with one word.

E: This is what Gina said after her exam.

Gina: ... about the sport famous in my country, I should have said things like, for example, every Sunday there are a lot of football games, and for example in Bogotá there, always there are two teams from each city and sometimes they, they start two teams playing and there is so interesting because there's a lot of people who goes to the stadium – and go and get fun, a lot of fun and there is a lot of people singing songs about one or the other team – and that's it, it's very interesting about football in my country, so I could say something else about that.

E: Another thing that helps is the use of 'fillers' – words we put in to give us time to think, like 'sort of' and 'you know'. Or 'anyway'. Now listen to Cat and Gina and let's see what kind of fillers they use.

E: Let's move on to talk about sport. How much time do you spend playing or watching sports?

Cat: In fact, I love swimming, but in the winter I come, so normally, I would do lots sport in summer, but not in winter.

E: How much time do you spend playing or watching sports?

Gina: Not at all, actually – I just play just a little tennis – I really don't like to watch sports, I don't like football or tennis so much.

I: I think Cat used 'in fact' and Gina used 'actually', didn't she?

E: Yes. However, 'fillers' are not always a good thing, not when they become mechanical, or sometimes their use is inappropriate. Look at these two examples of Ahmad using 'of course.

E: Do you think all children should do some sport?

Ahmad: Of course it's very necessary.

E: Why?

Ahmad: Because if you have a good condition you always

have some motivation, you should always be active to be healthy and, and to study better.

E: OK. Now I'm going to ask you about cooking. Do you like cooking?

Ahmad: Yes, of course. Sometimes I like to cook, but it is more, it's mostly is some fast food, have not enough time to cook too much.

E: The second use is inappropriate. Why should we suppose that he likes cooking? In the first example his vocabulary was rather good, though, for example he said 'motivation'.

IELTS Speaking Module: Part 2

E: In this part of the Speaking module, the examiner asks the candidate to talk for one or two minutes about a topic, usually something in the candidate's personal experience – something they've done or would like to do, somewhere they've been, someone they know, etc. The examiner gives the candidate a card with the topic written on it, with four points they must mention.

I: Does the candidate have any time to prepare their talk?

E: Yes, up to a minute to write some notes. Let's have a look.

E: In this part, I'm going to ask you to talk about a topic for one or two minutes. Firstly, you are going to have a chance to prepare your talk and write a few notes. Here's a piece of paper and a pencil for writing your notes. I'd like you to describe a shop that you enjoy going to.

E: The candidate has to say where the shop is, what it sells, how often he or she goes there. They also have to explain why they enjoy visiting it. This card is pretty clear but sometimes they might have to ask the examiner to explain something, like a word, or how exactly the task is supposed to be done.

I: So they should ask 'What does this word mean?' or something like that.

E: Yes, or 'So, can I talk about a market I visit at weekends?'

I: Anything that the candidate should keep in mind while writing notes?

E: Well, it's a good idea to write keywords – important vocabulary which the candidate can use during the talk. And let's see two examples of notes.

I: The second one's called a word web, isn't it?

E: Yes – not that you always have to write notes like that, but some candidates find it helps them to think of things to say.

I: Yes, it certainly looks better organised than the first one. And there are lots of keywords. Any other tips for when the candidate is actually speaking?

E: Yes, it's important to be quite natural and look at the examiner. Let's see how Cat does this.

E: All right? Remember you have one to two minutes of this, so don't worry if I stop you. Can you start talking now, please?

Cat: OK. I enjoy going to the shop – name's Top Shop – it's Oxford Street. I like to shop, I mean I like to shop in there because – how you say, is really fit for young person and they not very expensive – I can found anything there which I want: clothes, trousers, anything for the body.

I: Yes, she does smile a lot and there's good eye contact with you.

E: That's right. She's not very fluent, though, as there's a lot of stopping and starting. And, as far as vocabulary is concerned 'fit' is the wrong choice – it should be 'suitable'. Also, her notes aren't helping her much. They're not very well organised.

I: But she does keep going, doesn't she?

E: Yes, that's very important. Now look at Ahmad.

Ahmad: I'm going sometimes to bookshop in Oxford Street and this is books in almost every subject in life from science to cooking and from different kind of subjects.

I: Yes, he looks at you now and again but not really enough. And he's very serious! Can I see a candidate doing a whole Part 2?

E: Why not? Let's take Hwan. He's the one who did the word web.

E: Remember, you only have one to two minutes for this, so don't worry if I stop you. Would you like to start speaking now?

Hwan: I'm quite interested in sports shops – so I usually go to Nike Town in, in Oxford Circus. So there are lots of, there are lots of sports shops in Nike Town. I've never been, I've never seen something like Nike Town in Korea so I really prefer to visit, to see Nike Town, so, I usually, I usually buy some T-shirts from Nike Town and sometimes I bought trainer which I need to – in this time usually work quite long away, long time, so I usually I need to buy some comfortable trainers, so and – sometimes I need to buy two protector to my wrists – I have quite weak wrists, so I sometimes I bought the protector and football, yes and I go, I usually go there twice a month to buy some stuff – socks or trainer, T-shirts, yes.

E: All right, so when did you last go there?

Hwan: Last Sunday, I went there last Sunday and I bought some socks and protector for my wrist.

E: And do you like to go there by yourself or with someone else?

Hwan: I usually go to, with my friend – but I, if, when I go, go there with my friend, I can, I can speak lots of things, I can ask their, I can ask theirs opinion – something like that, but sometimes quite too uncomfortable – I have to follow theirs opinion or theirs way, but I prefer go to my friend.

I: You asked a couple of questions at the end.

E: Yes, these follow up questions are called 'bridging' questions, to enable us to move smoothly onto Part 3. His talk did seem well-organised. He mentioned everything on the card and had enough to say. As for his language, there were some pronunciation problems, such as a confusion between 'p' and 'f'. And his intonation was a bit flat. His vocabulary was a bit simple, though he did use one specialist word, 'protector'.

I: He kept repeating 'Nike Town'.

E: Yes, you need to connect your ideas, using pronouns like 'it' or 'there, or phrases like 'this shop'. That's part of coherence. Also, his grammatical range was rather limited, especially at the beginning. But his ability to organise his material was a positive point.

IELTS Speaking Module: Part 3

I: So what happens in the third part of the Speaking exam?

E: Well, like Part 1, it's a question-and-answer session, but it's more of a discussion, based on the topic of Part 2 – in this case, shopping. The candidate should be able to answer questions about society, the educational system, the environment, and so on.

I: Any advice?

E: Well, as in Part 2, if the candidate doesn't understand anything, they should ask the examiner to explain. Cat doesn't do this.

E: Are there certain kinds of shop that are becoming more popular?

Cat: Sorry? I'm not really understand.

E: Are there certain kinds of shop that people are going to more than they used to before?

Cat: Um ...

E: Do people enjoy shopping now in certain shops that they didn't go to before.

Cat: Sorry. I'm not really understand.

E: But Hwan does it rather well.

E: People say that this society we live in is very consumerist. Do you think that this brings any disadvantages?

Hwan: Consumerist, consumer?

E: Consumerism is when everything is directed towards buying. OK? We are encouraged to buy more and more and that is what people value. So, do you think this is a good or bad development?

Hwan: I think that is good for our economy – just, if we don't want to spend money our economy system is, will be stopped, so government should encourage to spend money to theirs people.

I: Yes, he responds immediately, whereas she just looked blank.

E: And he used a good conditional sentence, with 'if'. Fairly complex.

I: Good grammatical range!

E: Yes. There are also certain language skills that the candidate is expected to show, for example, to express an opinion, with an appropriate introducing expression such as 'I think', 'in my opinion', 'what I think is' and to support that opinion.

Gina: Yes, safer than if you pay by debit, but no I think, is there is not a disadvantage. I think it's good, I think it safer for everybody not to carry out but to carry their money inside the wallet

E: We are looking for wider vocabulary, not just 'I think', 'I think', 'I think', but 'in my opinion', 'in my view', 'I strongly believe' and so on. Another thing they may have to do is to evaluate – to express agreement or disagreement with someone else's ideas. So they should say 'I agree', 'I disagree, 'I don't think that's right', etc.

I: What other sorts of things do they have to do with their language?

E: Well, to compare and contrast. Let's look at Cat doing this.

E: Which is better do you think for shopping at – a small local shop or a large supermarket or department store?

Cat: I think it's the like the big shopping centre markets is much better than the small shop because we can find everything there we need, it include everything – and I think it's much cheaper than the small shops, special shops also, think, yeah.

E: Another thing candidates may have to do is to hypothesise, probably by using conditional sentences with 'if' and 'would' to describe an imaginary or improbable situation.

E: In this country, at any rate, it's pretty easy for people to get credit from their banks, etc. What would happen if it was suddenly made much more difficult.

Gina: Sorry?

E: What would happen if it were suddenly made much more difficult to get credit from banks?

Gina: I think the people will use the cash but the credit card is, you know – the people tend to buy more things than they need with a credit card, so if the banks doesn't have like facilities to get one credit card – the people wouldn't, wouldn't buy some things.

E: This response is good, using a lot of 'woulds' but it rather breaks down later.

I: Perhaps because she doesn't understand the question. You weren't asking just about credit cards, but what would happen if the banks refused all credit in general.

E: And candidates may also have to speculate, to

imagine what's going to happen in the future. Let's look at Cat's response to a question about the future of shopping.

E: Where do you think shopping will change in the future. Do you think shopping will change?

Cat: Online, yeah.

E: And is that a good or bad development?

Cat: Good, because it's easy and we save time, yeah, because, I don't know, my teacher, Joanna – she, she do shopping every week just online and book, and then they will just come and give you all things you book just a little bit and you really save your money and your time, because when we do shopping I think we two or three hours and she just maybe ten minutes, yeah.

E: This isn't really a sufficient response. It's good that she relates the future to the present but she seems to be just talking about the present. When speculating about the future, candidates should be using phrases like 'perhaps this will happen' or 'this will probably happen', and employ modal verbs, like 'may' or 'could', for example, 'cash may disappear one day'.

IELTS Speaking Module: Sample Interview

E: Now that we've looked at all three Parts separately, let's watch a whole speaking test from beginning to end.

This is Gina, and I'd like you to notice her very confident manner, and the way that she maintains eye contact at the right places, particularly on keywords or important words when she glances at the examiner. Also, ask yourself about the general points we mentioned at the beginning: is she fluent, is her speech well connected, does she use the right words and a fairly wide range of them? Does she make a lot of grammatical mistakes and does she use a wide range of grammatical forms? And what about her pronunciation? She obviously has a South American accent, but can she be understood most of the time?

I: Yes, and how well does she do those other things you mentioned, like expressing her opinion, hypothesising or speculating?

E: Good afternoon.

Gina: Good afternoon.

E: My name is Ranald Barnicot. Could you tell me your full name please?

Gina: My name is Gina Diaz.

E: Uh-huh. What should I call you?

Gina: Gina, please.

E: Where do you come from, Gina?

G: I'm from Colombia.

E: OK. I'm going to start by asking you some personal questions – some questions about yourself. First of all, where do you live in London?

Gina: I live near Caledonian Road – it is Middleton Road.

E: What kind of place do you live in?

Gina: Oh, what kind of?

E: What kind of place do you live in?

Gina: In a flat, with three flatmates.

E: What do you like best about where you live?

Gina: I think I feel lucky for where my home, because is, I have my own room, I have kitchen, I can cook and everything like that.

E: What kind of jobs do people do in your area?

Gina: Well there is like home, just homes in my area but maybe in Camden Town there is a lot of supermarkets and everything like that.

E: Would you say that London is a good place to study in?

Gina: Yeah, I think it's great and everything is so close to another place and the transport is so good.

E: OK, let's move on to talking about sport. How much time do you spend playing or watching sports?

Gina: Not at all, actually, I just play just a little tennis, and I really don't like to watch sports, I don't like football or tennis so much.

E: Which sports are most popular in your country?

Gina: Football.

E: Which sports did you do when you were at school?

Gina: Hmm, a little volleyball, just volleyball, basketball just a little bit.

E: Do you think all children should do some sport?

Gina: Yeah, I think I think this maintain far away from drugs and I think its good that they practice some kind of sport football or anything like that and it's good for the heart.

E: OK, I'm going to ask you about cooking now. Do you like cooking?

Gina: Yeah, but I don't know how to cook too much.

E: How often do you go to restaurants?

Gina: Here no, no, not too much but in Colombia I usually go to restaurants.

E: What kinds of restaurants do you enjoy eating in?

Gina: I love sushi, and I love steaks, and like that.

E: What does a restaurant need to do in order to be successful?

Gina: I think a good client services, I think is the best, and good food, of course.

E: OK. I'm going to move on now to the second part. In this part you have to talk about a topic for one or two minutes. Before you talk you'll have one minute to write some notes if you wish. Here's some paper and a pencil for your notes, and this is your topic. Describe a shop you enjoy going to.

E: All right? Remember you only have one or two minutes, so don't worry if I stop you. Can you please start talking now.

Gina: OK, in Colombia I love to go to one shop that's called Andino. Inside of this shop there was, there were a lot of little shops where you can buy clothes, shoes, and everything like that, jewelleries. Well, I usually go there almost all weekends and I love to go there because you can see all kind of things like clothes, jeans, shoes and everything like that. Also you can, you can see or you can stay in a restaurant to eat something and if you want you can stay to go to movies, because there inside that shop there is a cinema so you can choose what movie did you want to see to enjoy with your friends or to hanging out with everybody.

The shop is located like in the centre of the city in Bogotá and around the shop there is a good, there is a lot of good places like restaurants and everything like that, so if you go there you can, then you, after you go shopping you can stay in a restaurant or you can stay in a pub, to hanging out with your friends. I love that kind of things, actually.

E: And do you like to go there by yourself, or with someone else?

Gina: Actually, I don't like too much to go alone. I usually go with my boyfriend or with friends to see the things that they sell there.

E: OK, so we've been talking about a shop that you enjoy going to. I'm going to ask you some more general questions about this. So, in your opinion, which is better for shopping at, a small local shop or a large department store or supermarket?

Gina: I think its better a large department store, because you can choose whatever you want. If you go to one small, you have to choose the few things that are sold there, but if you go to a large department, you can choose all kind of brands and all kind of shoes, and I don't know, I think it is better a large one.

E: What do you think has been the effect of the growth of supermarkets and department stores on small shops?

Gina: I think because of the – I don't know how to say that – maybe because there is a lot of people with needs, different needs and you can go there in a big one and you can satisfy the customers with all kind of things, so you don't have to focus on just one client that want this kind of food or this kind of clothes. The big ones focus on all kind of clients so they can satisfy every needs that they want, that they have.

E: OK, what do you think of shopping centres? Do we need them?

Gina: Do we need them?

E: Do we need shopping centres?

Gina: Yeah, yeah, because you can enjoy yourself just to see what they are selling. You don't have to buy anything just have to see and you can enjoy, that's

because you need. You have to relax yourself, going there to see what maybe you can buy, maybe you haven't done, I mean, you wouldn't need to buy something, but if you're going to the shopping centre maybe you can buy something and this is good.

E: In your country, how do people choose to pay? Do they use cash or credit card, or debit card?

Gina: I think in the small ones the people pay by cash, but in actually in this moment I think that credit card and debit card is more used in this time than last time so I think, right now is better to pay by credit card and it's safer is more safe than to pay by credit or debit card is more used to credit card.

E: Can you think of any social disadvantages in the boom in the use of credit cards?

Gina: Maybe sometimes you can find some problems because there is not the line, or your credit card doesn't work so good so there is some restaurant that doesn't receive credit or debit card you have to pay by cash and then you have to walk up to the cash machine and get out the money and that could be, yes, less safe than if you pay by debit, but no, I think, there is not a disadvantage, actually, I think it's good, I think it safer for everybody not to carry out, carry their money inside the wallet, just to use your credit or debit card.

E: In this country, at any rate, it's pretty easy for people to get credit from their banks, etc. What would happen if it was suddenly made much more difficult.

Gina: Sorry?

E: What would happen if it was suddenly made much more difficult to get credit from banks?

Gina: I think the people will use the cash but the credit card is, you know – the people tend to buy more things than they need with a credit card, so if the banks doesn't have like facilities to get one credit card – the people wouldn't, wouldn't buy some things.

E: OK, suppose that you suddenly need quite a lot of money. How can you persuade your bank to lend you the money?

Gina: I think this is not easy because the bank never is going to lose her, its money, so you cannot persuade your bank, you just have to have the papers all the papers cleared like I know, credit history – how to say that – and statements and everything like that because there is no way that you say to the bank, 'oh please I need money, I need money', because the bank is not going to loan you money if you don't have the papers and, good I think, so ...

E: Thank you very much, that's the end of the Speaking test.

Gina: OK.

Overview

Watch the opening part of the video and answer the following questions about the exam.

1 How many parts are there to the Speaking module?

a 3   **b** 4   **c** 5

2 How long is it in total?

a 5–7 minutes   **b** 8–10 minutes   **c** 11–14 minutes

3 How many people will be in the interview room?

a 1 examiner/1 candidate   **b** 1 examiner/2 candidates   **c** 2 examiners/1 candidate

4 There are different criteria that the examiner will use to assess your performance. Listen to the examiner explain what you need to do to perform well in the exam and match the criteria to their definitions below.

CRITERION		DEFINITION
a Fluency and coherence	☐	**1** using correct grammar, including using a wide selection of grammatical forms
b Vocabulary	☐	**2** being able to produce correct sounds, with the appropriate stress, rhythm and intonation
c Accuracy and range of grammar	☐	**3** being able to use a relatively high number of words with the correct meaning and in the correct form
d Pronunciation	☐	**4** speaking naturally and without hesitation; not pausing too much, and speaking at the proper speed

Part 1

1 Write three examples of topics the examiner might ask about in Part 1.

....

2 Should candidates answer questions in Part 1 as briefly as possible?

   a yes **b** no

Giving extended responses

Watch three candidates answering an examiners questions in Part 1 of the exam and answer the questions that follow.

Cat

3 What additional information does Cat provide about her hometown? Tick (✔) all topics that she mentions.

   a her town's name ☐

   b its location ☐

   c the population ☐

   d what it's like ☐

Gina and Ahmed

4 Who gave an extended response to the examiner's question?

   a Gina   **b** Ahmed   **c** both   **d** neither

Using fillers

5 Give three examples of fillers mentioned by the examiner.

....

6 What fillers do the following candidates use?

   Cat ....

   Gina ....

7 Ahmed uses 'of course' as a filler twice.

   The first time it is used **appropriately/inappropriately.**

   The second time it is used **appropriately/inappropriately.**

8 What word that Ahmed uses does the examiner say is a good vocabulary item?

....

Pairwork

Now speak with a partner to ask and answer the following questions. Remember to use 'fillers' and to give extended answers.

Where do you come from?

How much time do you spend playing or watching sports?

Which sports are most popular in your country?

Do you think all children should do some sport?

Do you like cooking?

Part 2

1 In Part 2 of the exam, how long does each candidate have to talk for?
a less than 1 minute
b 1 to 2 minutes
c more than 2 minutes

2 What might a candidate have to talk about in this part? Tick the topics the examiner mentions.
a something the candidate has done ☐
b something in the news ☐
c a place the candidate has been ☐
d something the candidate would like to do ☐
e a person the candidate knows ☐

3 How long do candidates have to prepare for the talk?
a 1 minute maximum
b 1 to 2 minutes
c more than 2 minutes

Asking for clarification
4 Give two examples of ways of asking for clarification mentioned on the video.
a What does ....?
b .... a market I visit on weekends?

Writing notes
5 What is one advantage of using a word web?
....

Cat and Ahmed
6 Whose performance is stronger, Cat's or Ahmed's? List some reasons for this.
....
....
....

Hwan
7 Listen to Hwan's Part 2 talk. What are some good and bad points about his performance?
good points:
....
bad points:
....

8 What two bridging questions does the examiner ask Hwan?
a ....
b ....

9 What alternative words or phrases could Hwan have used to refer to Nike Town?
....

Pairwork

Now practise Part 2, using the Topic cards below. Firstly, spend one minute preparing by writing notes. Then, each speak for one or two minutes on the topic given. When your partner has finished, ask the bridging questions below.

Student A

Describe a restaurant or eating-place that you have visited.

You should say:
  where it is
  what kind of food it serves
  whether it is cheap or expensive
and explain what you liked or disliked about eating there.

Student B

Describe an item that you would like to buy.

You should say:
  what it is
  where you might buy it
  how much it might cost
and explain why you might want to buy it.

Bridging Questions
Student A
Ask student B:
  Have you always wanted to buy it?
  Will this product be popular in future?

Student B
Ask student A:
  Do you think you will go there in future?
  Do other people you know feel the same way as you about it?

Part 3

1 Part 3 of the Speaking exam is based on the topic of
   a Part 1   **b** Part 2.

2 What examples of Part 3 topics are given by the examiner?

....

....

3 According to the examiner, which candidate asks for clarification more effectively?
   a Cat   **b** Hwan

Expressing an opinion

4 What are some phrases the examiner gives for introducing an opinion?

....

Evaluating

5 What are some phrases the examiner gives for evaluating someone else's opinion?

....

Comparing and contrasting

6 What is Cat asked to compare and contrast?

....

Hypothesising

7 Hypothesis questions use words like .... and .... They ask about
   a real-life   **b** imaginary situations.

Speculating

8 What words or phrases to talk about the future are mentioned by the examiner?

....

Pairwork

Now ask each other the following questions that were on the video.

Are there certain kinds of shop that are becoming more popular?

Which is better for shopping at – a small local shop or a large supermarket or department store?

In your country, how do people prefer to pay – in cash or by credit card?

Can you think of any social disadvantages in the recent boom in the use of credit cards?

What would happen if it was suddenly made much more difficult to get credit from banks?

In what ways do you think shopping is going to change in the future?

People say that this society that we live in is very consumerist. Do you think that this brings any disadvantages?

Sample Interview

Watch Gina and evaluate her performance by circling the appropriate letter:
a = good; **b** = OK ; **c** = needs more work. Provide examples where possible.

				Reason(s) / Example(s)
Part 1				
Use of fillers	a	b	c	
Extended responses	a	b	c	
Part 2				
Interaction with examiner	a	b	c	
Request for clarification	a	b	c	
Organisation of talk	a	b	c	
Ability to keep going	a	b	c	
Part 3				
Understanding of questions	a	b	c	
Request for clarification	a	b	c	
Evaluation	a	b	c	
Comparing and contrasting	a	b	c	
Hypothesising	a	b	c	
Speculation	a	b	c	
In general				
Fluency and coherence	a	b	c	
Vocabulary	a	b	c	
Grammatical accuracy and range	a	b	c	
Pronunciation	a	b	c	

Pairwork

Use the questions from Parts 1, 2 and 3 to practise the entire interview in pairs. Assess your partner's performance according to the criteria in the table above.

SPEAKING VIDEO

Overview

1 a
2 c
3 a
4 a h; b g; c e; d f

Part 1

1 sport, travel, food, family life
2 no.
3 a; b; d
4 d
5 sort of; you know; anyway
6 Cat: in fact; Gina: actually
7 first time: appropriately; second time: inappropriately
8 motivation

Part 2

1 b
2 a, c, d, e
3 a
4 a this word mean; b Can I talk about
5 It helps candidates think of things to say.
6 Cat's is stronger, because she smiles a lot, has good eye contact and keeps going. Ahmad is too serious and doesn't have enough eye contact with the examiner.
7 Good points: well-organised; mentioned everything on card; had enough to say; one specialist word
Bad points: pronunciation (confusion between /p/ and /f/; flat intonation); simple vocabulary; limited grammatical range; poor coherence–repetition of *Nike Town*
8 a When did you last go there? b Do you like to go there by yourself, or with someone else?
9 it; there; this shop

Part 3

1 b
2 society; educational system; environment
3 Hwan
4 I think; in my opinion; what I think is; in my view; I strongly believe
5 I agree; I disagree; I don't think that's right
6 a small, local shop and a large supermarket or department store
7 if; would; b
8 perhaps this will happen; this will probably happen; may; could

Sample interview

Part 1

Use of fillers: b – actually, hmmm, of course
Extended responses: a – detailed and informative with the one exception referred to in the interview

Part 2

Interaction with examiner: a – smiles, good eye contact
Request for clarification: does not apply
Organisation of talk: a – deals with all task elements in turn and in sufficient detail
Ability to keep going: a – very little hesitation, some repetition, e.g. to hanging out with my friends

Part 3

Understanding of questions: c – on occasion at cross-purposes with examiner, e.g. did not understand question about social disadvantages of credit cards such as increase in debt
Request for clarification: b – did this by repeating examiner's question, e.g. *Do we need them?* and by *Sorry?*
Evaluation: does not apply
Introducing opinion: b – uses *I think* exclusively
Hypothesising: b – good attempt, but mixes up 1st and 2nd conditional, also doesn't understand examiner's question about credit
Speculation: does not apply

In general

Fluency and coherence: a – very good at this level, although there is occasional hesitation while searching for grammar/vocabulary, and at one point in Part 3, there is confusion between you for customer and you for supermarket manager as in: ... *and you can go there in a big one and you can satisfy the customers.*
Vocabulary: a – some quite specific vocabulary, e.g. *flatmate, client services, credit history, statements*
Grammatical accuracy and range: b – in general, an ambitious range of structures, with a lot of inaccuracies: omission of subject: *is better to pay by credit card*; subject – verb agreement: *this maintain*; active for passive: *one shop that calls Andino*; double subject: *it's better a large department store*;, incorrect conditional structures.
Pronunciation: a – recognisably foreign, but quite easy to understand, some errors in individual sounds, e.g, *chops for shops, vig* for *big*; intonation rather sing-song

Describe a visit to an art gallery, museum or important building.

You should say:
   where you went
   when you went there
   why you went there

and explain whether or not you enjoyed the experience.

Describe one of your favourite books.

You should say:
   what the book is
   who wrote it
   what the book is about

and explain why you enjoy this book so much.

Describe something you have done which makes you feel proud.

You should say:
   what you did
   when you did it
   how you did it

and explain why you feel particularly proud of this achievement.

Describe a favourite possession.

You should say:
   what this thing is
   how old it is
   where you got it from

and explain why you like this thing so much.

Describe a person you admire.

You should say:
  who this person is
  how old this person is
  what this person does

and explain why you admire them so much.

Describe a holiday you have enjoyed.

You should say:
  where you went
  when you went
  who you went with

and explain why the holiday was so enjoyable.

Describe a film, play, or concert you have recently seen and enjoyed.

You should say:
  what you saw
  when you saw it
  where you saw it

and explain why it was so enjoyable.

Describe a building which you particularly like.

You should say:
  what this building is
  where it is
  what it looks like

and explain why you like this building so much.